THE
BEST
SECRETS
OF GREAT SMALL
BUSINESSES

THE
BEST
SECRETS
OF GREAT SMALL
BUSINESSES

Creative, Innovative and Cost-Saving
Ideas from Great Business Minds

RAY SILVERSTEIN

SOURCEBOOKS, INC.®
NAPERVILLE, ILLINOIS

Published by Sourcebooks, Inc.
P.O. Box 4410, Naperville, Illinois 60567–4410
(630) 961-3900
FAX: (630) 961-2168
www.sourcebooks.com

Library of Congress Cataloging-in-Publication Data
Silverstein, Ray.
 The best secrets of great small businesses : creative, innovative, and cost-saving ideas from
great business minds / Ray Silverstein.
    p. cm.
 Includes index.
 1. Small business--Management. 2. Small business--Growth. I. Title.

HD62.7.S535 2006
658.02'2--dc22

                                                      2006019060

            Printed and bound in the United States of America.
                  POD 10 9 8 7 6 5 4 3

DEDICATION

This book is dedicated to my most influential teachers of life, business, and success—my parents: Harry and Connie Silverstein.

CONTENTS

ACKNOWLEDGMENTS

This book would not be possible without the support, innovative ideas, and concepts of members of PRO, President's Resource Organization. These business leaders have invested their time and money to help each other, but I have also learned a great deal. Thank you for bringing fresh perspective to small business opportunities and concerns.

I also owe a huge thanks to Joanne Levine who motivated, pushed, and cajoled me to do a book on peer advisory boards so others could learn some secrets of their success. I am also deeply indebted and owe a huge thanks to Julie Kramer who helped synthesize ideas and, for her wordsmithing. This book could not have been done without Julie.

I would also like to thank the staff of Sourcebooks for their support and help, especially Peter Lynch, Rachel Jay, and Scott R. Miller.

I am looking forward to continued learning of new secrets and great ideas from my friends and associates—PRO members.

INTRODUCTION

THE POWER OF PEER GROUPS

You'll find this book packed with hundreds of ideas, solutions, and strategies just for small business owners—all successfully tested and proven to work by real-life entrepreneurs.

WHERE DID ALL THESE CONCEPTS COME FROM?

This book represents just a sampling of ideas arising from discussions in numerous peer group advisory meetings—in this case, PRO (President's Resource Organization) meetings. Small peer group advisory boards are made up of small business leaders, such as company presidents, owners, CEOs, COOs, and partners. The groups consist of twelve members or less. Their businesses are generally of similar size or complexity, but in noncompeting industries.

Members gather each month to discuss business issues and challenges with their peers in a meeting led by a trained, experienced facilitator.

In a confidential setting, members give and receive objective input from others who walk in their shoes. They gain invaluable insights they can't receive from employees, outside professionals, or family members. Discussions are candid and free flowing, marked by camaraderie and synergy. Most PRO groups have been meeting since 1993, and many boast a number of original members.

What kinds of people belong to peer group advisory boards like PRO? People who answer yes to the following questions:

- Are you alone at the top?
- Do you feel you have no one to talk to about the pressures and decisions you face each day?
- Do you worry about working in your business rather than on your business?
- Are you hungry for new ideas and strategies?

If you answered yes to these questions, you might benefit from belonging to a business peer group. I've found that business owners who join peer groups often fit a certain profile—they want to grow their businesses, are eager to learn new information, and are willing to accept constructive criticism. They tend to be progressive and creative in the way they operate. They don't believe that they already know it all.

Belonging to an advisory board requires a time commitment, although it amounts to less than a round of golf per month. If you fit the profile, this may be time very well spent. As you will see, there are many advantages.

WHAT A PEER GROUP CAN OFFER YOU

An effective peer group offers its members a wide range of benefits, including the following:

The Feeling You're Not Alone at the Top

All business owners are in business *for* themselves, but with an advisory board they are not in business *by* themselves. Who do you talk to when you're dealing with gut-wrenching issues that keep you awake at night? If you belong to a peer group, that's who you talk to. That's where you go for resolution and support. A peer group is the outside board of directors you wish you had.

Insight

Diverse experience within the advisory board brings different cultures, backgrounds, and viewpoints to bear on any issue. As the head of your company, you are sometimes too close to issues to see the clear solution. A peer group can provide the objectivity you need.

Sounding Board

Go ahead, think out loud. A peer group is the place to air issues you can't discuss with employees and family. You will receive rational, unbiased feedback for even your wackiest ideas.

Knowledge

The average advisory board has more than two hundred years of business management experience. This experience translates to knowledge—the practical hands-on knowledge that comes from surviving similar situations. Remember, each advisory board is made up of people who have a diverse set of business skills; each brings unique knowledge to the table.

Creative Solutions and Ideas

Peer groups brainstorm together—a proven method of generating fresh solutions and ideas. Remember, advisory boards are composed of people who are entrepreneurial and creative in their outlook and who see things from various perspectives. Can you get such diverse thinking from your company's executive team members—all who operate from within the same environment? No!

Accountability

As business owner and president, you report only to yourself. A peer advisory board supplies that missing accountability. Join an advisory board, and your fellow members will consistently question you on your progress. It's pure peer pressure: business leaders don't want to look foolish; therefore, they will accomplish those difficult tasks. Both your facilitator and fellow members will hold your feet to the fire.

Less Troubleshooting Time

The opportunity to confront issues with your peers moves solutions to the forefront faster. Many times, a particular issue will be resolved for one member only to be encountered by another shortly after. Because this issue was already aired in a meeting, the member already knows how to resolve it—therefore saving time and peace of mind.

Think Tank

Think about it. If you were to hire the talent needed to solve all of your business problems, how much would it cost? Far more than any membership fees!

Support

Advisory board members receive support in both positive and negative situations. Say you have to cut your workforce—an unpopular, uncomfortable action. This is the only group that will understand your difficulty and applaud you for doing what is necessary. Without such motivation, business owners often delay taking negative actions, many times to the detriment of their companies. On the other hand, when a member makes a risky but positive decision (to make a hire or invest in equipment) it will be celebrated by his or her advisory board.

Connections

Peer groups are great resources for top professional help. Advisory board members help each other find outstanding bankers, lawyers, accountants, and insurance profession-als because they refer only people they trust. And there's another benefit here. Even though peer groups are not based on the idea of finding sales within the group, when people have confidence in each other, they want to do business together. And they do.

Unbiased Feedback

Are you willing to talk to your friends or family about delicate business problems—an alcoholic employee or a sexual harassment claim? Peer group members don't take ownership positions like employees do. They don't have the emotional involvement of family. Nor do they have a vested interest, like professional advisors do. Rather than a knee-jerk reaction, peer groups respond with thought-ful, objective suggestions.

Experienced Risk Consultants

Bankers, lawyers, and accountants are trained to elimi-nate risk, but business owners are trained to weigh and evaluate risk. If you're considering a risky venture, who could you count on for a balanced response?

Confidentiality

The cornerstone of any advisory board is confidentiality. Members can feel confident that their conversations will go no further than the four walls of the meeting room.

Camaraderie

A peer group is also a personal club. As members meet month after month, kinship develops. Members are coaches, mentors, advisors, and friends to each other.

OTHER TYPES OF BUSINESS GROUPS AND BOARDS

In addition to paid advisory boards, there are many types of business groups. The question is, what do they have to offer you and is it what you need? You can belong to multiple business groups and get different things from each of them.

Chambers of Commerce

Your chamber of commerce is a great place to network and to work on community matters. But this is not a group to confide in. These groups do not necessarily meet on a regular basis, create accountability, or use a facilitator to drive discussions to conclusion.

Trade Associations

These organizations are helpful for achieving certain "macro" industry goals, like developing product and government specifications or overall labor agreements. But again, this is not a forum for confidential issues. Would you ever discuss a quality issue, a customer problem, or a sticky personnel problem here? No!

Friends and Family

Your friends and family may not have the business experience required to resolve a business issue. In addition, there is a tendency to make these issues emotional rather than objective. In fact, such a discussion might generate more stress than you had in the first place!

Business Advisors, Like Lawyers and Accountants

As mentioned before, these professionals are trained to eliminate risk, not measure it. In addition, they are not generally sales or marketing driven, but technically driven. As technicians, they can't offer much insight when it comes to issues such as motivating employees or entertaining a new marketing program. They're excellent advisors—but only within specialized fields.

Industry-Specific Groups

Several business sectors, such as new car dealers and instant print shops, enable owners within the industry to meet quarterly. Generally, the members come from different geographical areas and therefore are not in direct competition. These groups examine details of their business sector, comparing financials, ratios, and best practices.

These groups are very beneficial if your industry offers one. But there is a downside: lack of innovation. Everyone is bathing in the same bathwater, so to speak. There are few novel ideas from outside the industry. And because only one member is allowed per area, the majority of owners are excluded from joining.

Board of Directors

In small businesses, the board of directors is usually the owner and his or her immediate family. Most corporations have boards of directors, but in most cases do not have outside board members.

Technically, the president reports to the board of directors. The board votes on issues such as the officers, the officers' compensation, and major corporate decisions. The president must abide by the board's decision. Small business owners don't want to report to anyone else, and therefore choose to become their own boards. This is understandable, but it eliminates the benefit of outside viewpoints, experience, and accountability.

Business owners who want the benefits of an outside board of directors normally have to pay board members a fee—sometimes up to $10,000 per year. Owners also have to provide director and officer liability insurance, which is costly and sometimes hard to obtain. But smart people will not serve on a board without such protection. And assuming you solve all that, how do you know who to ask to be on your board?

In contrast, a peer advisory board can serve as your board of directors, but without exerting any legal influence, wielding only the substantial power of peer pressure.

Volunteer Advisory Boards

Another option to a paid board of directors is to create a voluntary board. Once again, you have to figure out who should serve on your board.

There are a few major limitations. In creating a voluntary board, you take on all responsibility of creating the agenda, getting the support materials, and conducting the meeting. In order to be effective, discussions must be unbiased and robust, which is no given thing. Furthermore, because volunteers are doing you a favor, it is sometimes hard to coordinate their time.

Because of the difficulty of setting an agenda and creating a meeting schedule, voluntary boards tend to lose their emphasis and consistency. They require real commitment, especially on behalf of the owner. And of course there is the perception that you get what you pay for. If there is no payment, what can the value be?

WHAT'S DIFFERENT ABOUT PAID PEER GROUPS

That brings us back to paid advisory boards, such as PRO. There are a number of such organizations, each with different features, benefits, and investments. If you're looking to join one, pick the one with features that best fit your schedule and budget. Most important, pick one that will give you the kind of results you need.

One of the unique benefits of paid advisory boards is that the members demonstrate a greater commitment. It only makes sense—they are putting their money where their mouth is, and they are looking for value too.

Another unique benefit is that members enjoy the services of a professional facilitator. The facilitator is the heart of the group, who questions, challenges, synthe-sizes, and elicits member participation.

The facilitator's role is to generate ideas and lead discussions to conclusion. The facilitator ensures that no one dominates the meetings. He or she will ask the tough questions and nip lengthy "war stories" in the bud. The facilitator acts as a connector to the business community, providing resources to members when needed. The facilitator also handles all the logistics and administrative activities, freeing members to focus on the issues that concern them.

When evaluating a prospective paid peer group, pay close attention to the facilitator. Do you think he or she has something to teach you? Do you respond to what he or she has to say? (In PRO, I require that all facilitators have already proven themselves as successful business leaders. They are not educators or theorists, but hands-on practitioners. They know what they're talking about—and the members respect them for it.)

The facilitator is the mentor and tormentor of the peer group. Every idea in this book arose from facilitator-led peer group meetings. And even though you may have missed the meetings, you don't have to miss out on the peer group discussion. That's why I wrote this book.

HOW TO USE THIS BOOK

What's the best way to use this book? There are a number of ways—as a problem solver, idea generator, or training tool, for starters. My hope is that you'll use it in the manner that is most helpful to you at any given time.

Your Daily Insight

Under ordinary circumstances, you can review an idea or two each day, then mull over ways these suggestions are best applied to your situation. Consider it your daily dose of insight! The book is organized into short, easy-to-read segments. Take it along to read on the train or while waiting for a meeting.

Idea Generator/Action Generator

Eager to grow? Use the ideas and examples in this book to help you brainstorm new approaches and strategies on nearly any aspect of your business.

Problem Solver

When you're having a specific problem—hiring a salesperson or evaluating employee performance—consider this your reference tool. The table of contents and index are designed to help you locate specific solutions to common small business challenges.

See Where You Stand: Using the Diagnostic Tests

Ready to identify opportunities for improvement? Take the diagnostic tests in chapter 10. After you've tabulated your results, consult that chapter to address your concerns. With some direction and determination you can turn those weaknesses into strengths!

Training Tool

This is also designed as a management training tool.

Some ideas are presented in the form of group dialogues; let your managers recreate them to stimulate thinking and sharing.

Contingency Planning

The point of this book is to make you think. Use it in good times and bad as a source for solutions or as a spark of inspiration.

CHAPTER ONE

THE BUSINESS OWNER'S ROLE/MANAGEMENT STRATEGIES

It's one thing to start a business; it's quite another to keep it growing. At some point, it's no longer enough to be your company's number one employee. You need to be the boss.

One of the great ironies of entrepreneurship is that it's not enough to be good at what you do. To grow your company, you must also be a good leader, goal setter, delegator, motivator, and visionary. Somewhere along the way, you must move your thinking from "me" to "us."

Like caterpillars transforming into butterflies, entrepreneurs must evolve into leaders if their companies are to grow. Let the metamorphosis begin!

RESPONSIBILITIES

When you take on the role of company leader, your responsibilities get bigger. You have a responsibility to your customers, employees, and community. Your job is to create a corporate vision and plot a strategy for achieving it. It's up to you to determine what risks are worth taking. And only you can craft your company's culture, setting its ethical and moral compass.

What Is My Role?

As their small businesses grow, many owners struggle to define their shifting roles within the organization. It's a given that many business owners are great doers. After all, they've built successful businesses from the ground up. But as a business takes off, owners are suddenly confronted by tasks outside their skill set, such as hiring staff and creating administrative policies.

For many, this can be an uneasy process. But in order to grow, an owner must be willing to operate outside his or her comfort zone. He or she must make the transition from *doer* to *thinker*—i.e., from working *in* the business to working *on* the business.

A number of PRO members have hired top managers to fill their shoes, only to find themselves asking, "Now what do *I* do? What is *my* role?"

The answer is deceptively simple. As chief executive, your role is to keep a finger on the pulse of the business. It is to recognize opportunity when it presents itself, formulate company strategy, and make sure that you have the right people in place to seize those opportunities and implement those strategies.

One PRO member who wrestled with this issue ultimately hired a president to replace himself. Now the owner serves as chairman. He sums up his current role this way: "My job is to make sure the process we use can be repeated."

You do not want to base future success on a fluky business strategy or a superstar employee. Your role is to dissect the ingredients of your company's success and ensure the processes are repeatable.

That's not all. Your role is to create your company's culture. Is it a formal environment? A creative one? Is it one in which employees are encouraged to take risks or follow rules? More important—what kind of culture *should* it be?

Often, a company's culture evolves haphazardly, springing from the founder's personal style. But as your company grows, it's wise to step back and evaluate the type of culture that is most likely to foster productivity and ensure success. If necessary, you can tweak your corporate culture to better serve your goals.

And obviously, it is your goal—always—to provide leadership. That means formulating strategy and communicating it clearly. Never assume your staff knows what you're thinking. You'll find more about leadership later in this chapter.

CASE STUDY: BILL

Bill, a longtime PRO member, owns a small, steadily growing telecommunications company. About a year ago, Bill hired a general manager to take over day-to-day administrative responsibilities.

The general manager has worked out nicely, freeing Bill from the myriad daily activities of running a company. But with all this found time, what is Bill's new role?

These days, Bill is staying abreast of developments in his fast-moving industry. This better allows him to create innovative new strategies that will *keep* his company growing down the road.

In addition, Bill retained responsibility for hiring the staff with the talent to implement his bold new strategies. Bill has successfully shifted his role from doer to thinker.

Measuring Risk: Don't Be a "Seymour"

Being in business means taking risks. As an established business owner, your job is to measure risk. That means reviewing possible actions and asking questions such as: What is the probability of success? Is this a risk I can afford to take?

When you first started your business, you willingly embraced some rather sizable risks. But here's the problem: the longer you are in business, the more risk-adverse you are likely to become.

When you started your business, you had less to lose. Along with success comes a sense of caution, a natural inclination to eliminate risk. Don't give in to it! That task belongs to your attorney and accountant—skilled technicians who are extensively trained to eliminate risk. When you start thinking like they do, your company will begin to decline. This is a sign that your company is approaching the end of the business life cycle.

If you want to keep growing, you need to keep your edge. That means you must continue taking risks. Evaluate them intelligently, but don't turn the evaluation process into a reason for stalling.

In business, you cannot expect to obtain all the data needed to make a hundred-percent foolproof decision. You cannot delay taking action forever because you want to "see more" facts and information. In other words, don't be a "Seymour."

Instead, follow the advice of legendary business expert Tom Peters: "Ready, fire, aim!" Okay, that's a bit of an overstatement. The point is, what you don't want to do is: "Get ready...aim...check your sites...check the wind...aim again...check the elevation...and fire." Why? Because by the time you finally squeeze the trigger, your target will be long gone.

One of the advantages of small business is flexibility. One of the disadvantages of small business is flexibility. Take charge of your flexibility—and accept that risk is part of growing a business.

Crafting a Corporate Culture

What's your company's corporate culture? Are you formal or informal? All business or somewhat playful? Is your company participatory or are you a benevolent dictator?

Perhaps you haven't given it much conscious thought. And that's just the point—it's time you did. In most small businesses, the company's culture evolves directly from the founder's personality. So if you wear a suit to work every day, chances are your employees do too. If you're a practical joker, chances are your office is ringing with laughter.

Take stock of your company culture. Does your existing culture contribute to your success—or does it detract from it? For example, one of our PRO members owns a company that he built from the ground up. As a result, his corporate culture was rooted in established allegiances and unwritten rules. In the beginning, this informal approach worked well for the company.

Over time, however, it became apparent that some long-term employees were contributing less and less—basically riding on the coattails of their past successes. With help from his fellow PRO members, the owner came to the reluctant conclusion that a change was in order. It was time to transition to a more performance-based culture—one that rewarded employees for delivering results.

Another PRO member, the owner of a small marketing company, has carefully cultivated an informal culture. She finds it encourages creativity, provides flexibility, and keeps morale high in a stressful, deadline-driven industry.

The point is, whatever your corporate culture is, it should not be accidental. Choose it, craft it, or change it so it works best for your company.

MANAGEMENT STYLES

Style is a matter of personality and personal taste, and that applies to management style, too. Whether you're a "benevolent dictator" or a "chameleon," every management approach has its pros or cons. There is no single right or wrong answer. The key is to know what your particular style is and to surround yourself with people who respond to that approach—and who share your ethics and beliefs.

RIDING THE HORSE VS. DRIVING THE TEAM

One of the toughest transitions for business owners is making the move from *doer* to *leader* as their companies expand. One of our PRO members compares this to horseback riding. Most small business owners are excellent horseback riders—but that does not automatically provide the skills needed to drive a team.

If you want your company to grow, you need to get off that horse and take over the reins of the team. If it doesn't come naturally to you, take lessons. Practice. Find proficient leaders and watch them in action. Or hire a pro that can drive the team for you. And of course make sure you have the right horses—horses that are willing to work together.

As your company grows, your task is to keep your team moving in sync. After all, what's more dangerous than a team of runaway horses?

The Chameleon Effect

In most small businesses, employees make the defining difference. So how do you maximize your employees' performance? How do you get key players and potential stars to perform to the best of their abilities?

One thing we've realized at PRO is that the majority of business owners tend to manage everyone the same way. The boss sets the tone and employees are expected to adjust accordingly. In other words, most owners have a distinct management style, just as their companies have their own corporate culture.

But is a single management style the best way to get the most from all your employees? After all, people are different. A challenge that motivates one person may discourage another. That's why, when it comes to management style, good managers advocate the Chameleon Effect.

Consider the clever chameleon—a master in the art of adaptation. This ancient lizard has one very effective survival tool: it changes color in response to its environment. It can shift from green to brown to red to yellow, depending on where it is and what it wants. Chameleons are experts at adapting to any given situation, a trait that savvy managers can adopt.

You start by looking at each employee individually. You assess their personalities, wants, and needs. You'll recognize that some people require handholding and close attention, while others thrive in a freer environment. Then you tailor your management style to best motivate each individual.

One human resources tool you might want to utilize here is the personality profile. This can tell you what makes each employee tick—and that factor alone is the key to effective management.

According to Dr. Richard Farson, renowned psychologist and management consultant, in his book *Management of the Absurd: Paradoxes in Leadership*, "Leadership is situational, less a personal quality than specific to a situation. True leaders are defined by the groups they are serving and they understand the job as being interdependent with the group."

Remember, it is easier for you to change than to make your employee change for you. In sales, you work to understand each of your customer's needs in order to satisfy them. Why not take the same approach with your employees?

"Let Chaos Reign…Then Rein in Chaos"

"Let chaos reign…then rein in chaos." So advises Andy Grove, founder of the wildly successful Oracle Corporation. It's good advice all right, but what does it mean? It means that order springs from chaos, just as surely as day follows night—a rule that applies to business as well as to the physical world.

What is chaos? Chaos is the infinite range of possibilities that face the entrepreneur. Say for example that you want to enter a new market. How do you start prospecting? Through telemarketers? Direct mail? Salespeople? With all these choices, how do you make an intelligent decision? You do so by evaluating each possibility in terms of your goal. Before you can transform chaos into order, you must have a carefully defined goal.

It's not much different than organizing a closet. Say your goal is a neat, easy-to-access supply closet. What do you do? First, you take everything out. You look it over. Then, you start putting things in piles according to kind: files over here, pens over there, sticky notes in the corner.

In other words, you compare the attributes of the various items and group them accordingly. Then, true to your goal, you start returning these newly categorized items onto the closet shelves, so they will be easy to find when you need them.

How do you translate that to business? Many small businesses get very involved—perhaps too involved—with tactics, particularly marketing activities. But before you can develop a tactic, you need to state your goal and then evaluate your options in terms of that goal. If you want to enter a new market, you need to first understand that market. Who are your customers? What is the best way to reach them? Answering those questions will help you impose order over chaos.

One of our PRO members, Bob, has a company that manufactures corrugated boxes. But the world of corrugated box buyers is vast indeed. How could Bob possibly market his products to such an enormous universe? Bob couldn't. Instead, he took inventory of his current customers, searching for commonalities. He realized he had several customers in the tuxedo industry. Why? Because one of the boxes he offers is a wardrobe with a hanging bar—perfect for keeping tuxedos wrinkle-free.

Bob then knew he had something the tuxedo industry wanted, and that knowledge gave him a focus for his marketing efforts. Bob shrunk the vast universe of possibility down to a manageable size. As a result, Bob developed a direct marketing program targeted to tuxedo retailers. He began attending tuxedo industry trade shows, positioning his company as a specialist. His efforts have paid off handsomely.

So chaos is good, but order is necessary if you are to navigate successfully through the business universe.

Are You a Benevolent Dictator?

What kind of boss are you? There are many management styles—a wide spectrum that ranges from fully participatory leadership to unyielding dictator.

Many small business owners find themselves playing the role of benevolent dictator. The boss rules, but he or she rules with heart and humanity. Is that good or bad?

Unfortunately, there is no definitive answer. But I can assure you that PRO members have dedicated hours to understanding various management styles and their impact on employees. And I can offer you a few observations, based on our groups' collective experience.

The benevolent dictatorship seems to work better in smaller organizations, where the business has a family feel. The bigger a company becomes, the greater the need for participatory leadership. After a certain point, an owner can no longer make every decision—he or she must be willing to relinquish authority and responsibility to qualified employees.

Some employees enjoy working for a benevolent dictator because they never have to make the tough decisions. Others chafe under such tight restrictions, especially those who have their own ideas.

Take Louis, for example. This benevolent dictator owns a car dealership and also has a son in the business. Louis decided to go into semiretirement and so he turned the reins over to his son James. While Louis was relaxing in Florida, James made substantial changes to the dealership, which he felt needed modernization.

What happened when Louis returned six months later? Louis was shocked and appalled, of course. He immediately set out to change everything back to its original state. Louis was suffering from Founder's Fault—the inability to yield responsibility along with authority. It's a common condition, and every business owner should know if he or she is prone to it.

As far as the best management style, there is no right or wrong. The point is to know what your style is and to surround yourself with people who are in tune with it. You don't want unhappy, unproductive, or out-of-control employees.

Know yourself, and know those who work for you.

CASE STUDY: JULIE

Julie, the owner of a chain of bridal stores, is a benevolent dictator. While this creates a family feel in her company, it also lands her in some sticky situations.

Rather than use a formula for calculating year-end bonuses, Julie awards bonuses based on personal decisions. Last year was very profitable for her company. Feeling generous, she gave her chief operating officer a large bonus equal to 20 percent of her salary. This year, although revenues are high, profits are down. Now Julie plans to scale bonuses back considerably. However, the COO—who is not privy to profit numbers, only revenues—is expecting another big bonus. Julie knows the COO will be disappointed and angry, yet she can't afford another giant bonus.

Now what? Because she doesn't have a bonus formula to point to, Julie is going to look like the proverbial bad guy.

The moral of the story is that being a benevolent dictator has pros and cons. One of the cons is it can get you into trouble!

Stop the Bus! Giving Non-Performers a Transfer

Firing an employee is one of the hardest tasks facing the small business owner. The job is so unpleasant that the world has created a gentle euphemism for it: "letting people go." Some PRO members also call it "giving out bus transfers."

Transferring riders off your bus is tough. But unless you're satisfied with mediocrity, you need to be willing to hand out those transfers when necessary.

Sometimes a long-term employee doesn't grow along with the business and the entire company pays the price. When this happens, you need to do one of two things: either find a new position for that employee—something he or she can excel at—or terminate him/her. It's a hard truth, but true nonetheless. And it's especially important when the economy is tight or when your company is struggling.

According to PRO members, one of the advantages of belonging to a peer group advisory board is that your fellow members will pressure you into performing the difficult tasks. Your peers will kindly cajole, nag, and badger you until you take the necessary action.

If you were a PRO member with a non-performing employee, your fellow members would remind you that you can't afford to carry dead weight. They would tell you that you need to jettison the non-performer so you can bring more quality people on board. And they would remind you that—in the long run—you are perhaps doing that non-performing employee a good turn. Being in the wrong job is a hardship. Such change isn't just good for the company, it may eventually be good for the employee, too—although it probably won't feel that way at the time.

Remember: it's your bus and it's up to you to keep it rolling. Be ready to hand out those transfers when necessary.

What's Your Company's Driving Force?

Do you know what drives your company? Many small business owners don't. Yet understanding what drives your firm can help you make better business decisions, from hiring the right people to implementing marketing programs to deciding how to spend your money.

A company can be driven by efficiency, technology, sales, cost, knowledge—any number of qualities. For example, a manufacturing company may be driven by the need to operate ultra-efficiently, boosting profits by keeping costs down.

Many small businesses are relationship driven. Their emphasis is on marketing, sales, and service—in other words, interacting with customers. If you don't know what drives your company, ask yourself: What single thing do we do best? Chances are that is what drives your operation.

As business becomes increasingly more competitive, knowledge becomes an increasingly important driver. Take Susan, a PRO member who owns a small advertising agency. Although her staff is very small, her company does a tremendous volume of business. Why? Because Susan has knowledge. Susan is a master at outsourcing. Her Rolodex is overflowing with the names of quality designers, copywriters, photographers, and media experts. When it comes to getting a project completed on time, she knows just who to call. Susan's company is knowledge driven.

Remember that quotation by Peter Drucker that I cited earlier? It's worth hearing again: "From now on, the key is knowledge. The world is becoming not labor intensive, not energy intensive, but knowledge intensive." Knowledge is invaluable, and that includes self-knowledge. Know thyself. And make a point of knowing what drives your organization.

LEADERSHIP

We all agree that "true leadership" is necessary to a company's survival. But what exactly does that mean? In my experience, leadership creates the rules and outcome of the game. The leader is head coach, player, and referee.

True Leadership Means Breaking the Status Quo

The world is moving more quickly than ever. In business and society, the rate of change is occurring faster than any time in human history. Machiavelli—a relentless strategist if ever there was one—once said, "Whoever desires constant success must change his conduct with the time." Five hundred years later, that observation is perhaps more relevant than ever.

Here's an example. Just a few years ago, a PRO member raised this question at one of our meetings: "Who is surfing the Net?" Most people in the room answered, "What's the Net?" Needless to say, we have come a very long way in a very short time. Today, the Internet and e-commerce are simply part of life.

If you're like most people, you went into business because you are good at whatever it is you do. Well, you may be the greatest computer programmer or salesman or whatever you are...but once you're in business, you need more than your own individual skills to survive. And if you're like most small business owners, you no longer have time to do those very things that you are good at. In order to survive and grow, you must become a student of change.

Today we see rapid change in distribution, products, service, technology, and attitudes. Does your business position itself to take advantage of these changes? Do you make forays into the world outside your business, observing changes and trends? And then use that information to reposition your business?

As a leader, it is your job to guide your company into new and unfamiliar territory—no matter how uncomfortable it may feel.

All businesses share one strategic direction today: to work in shorter time frames. Many PRO members are reinventing themselves to take advantage of the current market...and to survive.

As a small business owner, you have a responsibility to your employees, family, and yourself to start thinking beyond your past experience. Imagine that your company existed in the early 1900s. Perhaps you manufacture buggy whips. One day, an upstart named Henry Ford shows up with this incredible horseless carriage. Your managers don't notice—they are busy supervising the production of buggy whips. But as company leader, it's your job to notice. And it's your job to determine that the time has come to stop making buggy whips and perhaps start making horns.

The old rule "if it ain't broke, don't fix it" no longer applies. In what seems like a heartbeat, your business can degenerate from a well-oiled machine to a well-oiled machine producing parts without a market. It is the leader's job to make sure that never happens, by constantly defying the status quo.

The School of Total Quality Management has this basic rule: *improving performance never ends.* Even if you are doing something well, you can always do it better. This requires constant awareness, an open mind, and a willingness to change.

IMPROVING INTERNAL COMMUNICATIONS

Collaboration is the key to a vibrant, smoothly running organization. But that can't occur without open communication. So it looks like those dreaded staff meetings are here to stay. Here are some ways to make them more productive.

Not Another Meeting or How to Make Meetings More Meaningful

Does anyone really enjoy attending meetings? Probably not. Many workers—both managers and employees—feel that meetings are a waste of time, that meetings don't help them meet their goals. Often meetings don't start on time, don't have a clear direction, and, worst of all, don't result in any meaningful conclusion.

It doesn't have to be that way—in fact, it shouldn't be that way. I offer you PRO's Rules of Engagement for Meaningful Meetings:

RULES OF ENGAGEMENT FOR MEANINGFUL MEETINGS
1. The meeting must start precisely on time (whether everyone is there or not).
2. The meeting must have a clearly stated objective.
3. The meeting must have a written agenda, identifying topics to be covered.
4. The meeting must have a formal schedule—and participants must adhere to it. Each portion of the agenda should be allotted a specific amount of time.
5. Responsibility for each portion of the agenda should be assigned to one or more attendees in advance.
6. The meeting should end with a formal, stated conclusion.

Some meetings are purely informational, but most are action oriented. Such meetings should conclude with the identification of the next steps, the assignment of specific responsibilities, and a timeline for achieving them.

In addition to the previous rules, some PRO members have devised some intriguing strategies for getting the most from their company's internal meetings. Consider these:

- *The Monday Morning Meeting: Stand Up and Be Timed!* William holds a managers' meeting every Monday at 7:30 a.m. Managers are expected to share their goals and activities for the week. To create a sense of urgency, attendees stand in a circle formation. An egg timer is passed from manager to manager, and each must complete his or her report before the timer runs out. This forces all speakers to arrive prepared. It also creates a sense of camaraderie. Even William, the president, reports in this manner.

- *The 8:37 a.m. Meeting.* Do you have problems starting meetings on time because employees don't show up promptly? Linda combats this widespread problem by scheduling all meetings at precise, unusual times—like 8:37 a.m. or 2:06 p.m. The meeting begins as scheduled, regardless of who is there, and information is not repeated. If an employee arrives late, it's his or her responsibility to find out what they missed. Why should others waste valuable time because someone else is tardy?

- *Using Peer Pressure: Who's Got the Clock?* Peer pressure is a terrific motivator. Joe purchased a large clock that is in attendance at every company meeting. When someone arrives late, the clock becomes that employee's albatross. He or she must carry it to future meetings and keep it on their desk at all times until the next person is late for a meeting. Then the clock is passed along.

- *Musical Chairpersons.* Do you lead all your meetings? If so, you may find that you do all the talking while your people passively listen. For this reason, a number of PRO members put various employees in charge of meetings, even rotating the designated chairperson.

This encourages others to speak up and get involved. It also helps fresh ideas surface. (But be careful not to run the meeting from the sidelines. As the boss, you are by nature intimidating. If you react negatively to your employees' ideas, they may be afraid to share them.)

Meetings should be productive, not counterproductive. Take steps to make your meetings more "meetingful."

DELEGATION

You can't grow your business all by yourself. You have employees, and you need them to get things done. Remember, your role is working *on* the business, not *in* the business. That means mastering the fine art of delegation.

Delegation, Not Abdication

If you're going to grow your company, you must delegate responsibility. But be careful to remember that delegation doesn't become abdication. Some managers struggle to find the line between the two. Delegating, in its true form, means turning over responsibility for a project or action without relinquishing overall responsibility for the results.

How do you delegate? The key is communication, as well as having confidence in the person you are delegating to. When delegating a task to an employee, you must define the objective and scope of the action to be taken (and that includes the employee's responsibility to report back to you). In other words, establish a defined reporting loop.

Be sure your discussion covers each of the following topics:

- The project's objective.
- Your vision of what a "good job" will look like.
- The degree of responsibility you're giving the employee in order to accomplish the project (be specific and give examples if necessary).
- The degree of authority you're giving the employee in order to accomplish the project (ditto the above).
- The timing of the project.
- The total budget for the project.
- Reporting criteria, including how often to report, what the report should cover, and the method of communication the employee should use.

Delegate and you're much more likely to get the results you want. Abdicate and what you get is anyone's guess.

Your Aging To-Do List

Some things—wine, cheese, beef—benefit from the aging process. Unfortunately, your to-do list isn't one of them.

Many PRO members have complained about the difficulty of keeping their to-do lists current. One PRO member, David, came up with a clever solution. When David adds a new item to his to-do list, he also marks the date it hit the list. Should an item remain untouched on his to-do list for thirty days, he delegates it. Perhaps the employee who receives the project isn't as qualified as his boss. That's okay with David because, to his way of thinking, some action is better than none at this point.

Look at it this way: if an item remains on your to-do list for an entire month, perhaps you should reexamine its importance. Clearly, it's not a priority. Is it really worth doing? And if so, are you the right person to do it?

Here's another tip: major, multistep projects don't belong on your to-do list. Instead, limit yourself specifically to the next step that will move you toward the project's completion. For example, "reduce expenses" does not belong on your to-do list. "Call XYZ vendor to renegotiate shipping expenses" does.

Your to-do list can be kept current if you limit it to specific, doable actions—not wishful thoughts and overarching goals. It's a tool like any other; keep it sharply honed so it works efficiently for you.

Don't Do Well What You Shouldn't Do at All

Yes, delegating work is a tricky business. Many PRO members admit it's difficult for them, usually for one of two reasons: either they enjoy the work and want to do it themselves, or they're convinced no one else can do the job as well.

Either way, failing to delegate to your employees is a bad habit that can ultimately stunt your company's growth. After all, your job is to perform big-picture activities that propel your company forward. (See "What is My Role?" on page 16.)

When a PRO member tells me he or she is "too busy" to attend a PRO meeting, I usually wonder if they are delegating enough of their work. I ask them what it is they'll be doing in lieu of coming to the meeting. Is it more important than the long-term health of the company?

There's an old adage that suggests that you should hire people who are better than you. Delegation is healthy for your entire organization—it broadens your employees' skills and helps them grow into increased responsibilities and levels of authority. When your employees grow, your company will too.

CASE STUDY: HENRY

Henry owns a sheet metal company that he inherited from his father. He grew up in the business and has great affection for it.

Henry's favorite activity is hanging out on the shipping dock, loading the trucks like he did as a teenager. He gets satisfaction from watching his products go out the door. But while Henry is busy loading the trucks, who is running the business and planning the company's future? Henry just might be the company's most efficient dockworker. The problem is, his title is president.

GOAL SETTING AND PERFORMANCE EVALUATION

In many small companies, there is a tendency *not* to measure employee performance or overall performance. And while that may work for a short while, ultimately if you can't measure it, you can't manage it. Creating measurements is critical to long-term success.

Goal Setting: The Key to Performance Evaluation

How do you measure performance? Through goal setting and standards. You may be surprised to learn that while most employees want to do a good job, many don't know exactly what's expected of them. Through standards, you tell your employees how that "good job" is defined in precise terms.

The vast majority of jobs are measurable, although some (like sales) are more obvious than others. PRO members unanimously recommend setting goals and standards for each area of your organization. Address one area at a time, starting with the most measurable, like sales or operations.

How do you set effective goals? Use the SMART definition. Goals must be:

- S—Specific
- M—Measurable
- A—Achievable
- R—Realistic
- T—Timely

For example, take your financial department. You might measure your employees by the timeliness of their financial reports, the deviations from budget on payroll, and the number of adjustments made by outside auditors upon review. All these measurements help you assess the job your people are doing.

When implementing goal setting for the first time, you may worry about your employees' acceptance of the idea.

Will they feel threatened? There are several things you can do to obtain their buy-in. First, ask for their input. Ask them for their definition of a "good job." Tell them that the goals set must be agreed to by both of you. Then remind them that you can't implement a viable incentive system until you can measure performance. For employees, goal setting and standards represent the opportunity to be rewarded for their efforts. For you, goal setting is a way to evaluate performance and then maximize it.

MISCELLANEOUS MANAGEMENT STRATEGIES AND IDEAS

One of the benefits of advisory boards is that you never know what you'll learn from your peers. Here is a potpourri of ingenious ideas that have worked for others. These don't neatly fit in any given category, but they're too good to pass up.

An Alternative to the "Noncompete" Contract

The traditional noncompete contract stipulates that salespeople cannot take an employer's clients with them if they leave the company. The contract stipulates that the salesperson and client cannot do business together for a certain period, usually for two or three years.

While that may work just fine for you, it doesn't hurt to consider alternative options. After all, such contracts aren't generally popular with sales professionals, who may be reluctant to sign them. Furthermore, these contracts are very difficult to enforce after the fact.

As an alternative to a noncompete contract, consider an arrangement that allows ex-salespeople to take your clients with them—provided they pay you handsomely for the privilege! I call this the "300% Compete Contract."

The contract reads like this: should an employee leave and lure your client away, that employee agrees to pay 300 percent of the client's billing. (In reality, sometimes the client will pick up the tab. No matter; either way, you get paid.) Not only are salespeople more willing to sign these kinds of contracts, they're infinitely easier to enforce. It's easy to prove the financial value of a client's billing, and it alleviates a great deal of the emotional upheaval that usually accompanies this situation.

The "300% Compete Contract" may sound radical, but it's also a practical solution to an age-old problem. Look at it this way: if an employee wants to leave, you're going to lose him or her anyway. Why not say good riddance...and receive a generous compensation for your loss?

When Employees Are Hired Away by Customers

Have you ever had a good employee hired away from you by one of your customers? How did it feel? What, if anything, did you do about it?

Some PRO members—particularly those with service firms, such as CPAs—don't mind it. They actually think it's a good thing, because it solidifies the customer relationship, creating a tie between the two firms. But most find it maddening. Not only do you lose a trained employee, you lose the customer, because now that employee will perform the work directly for their new employer.

That's how PRO member Kathy felt after losing one of her best graphic designers to a key client. Kathy, after sharing her frustration with her PRO board, vowed never to be taken by surprise again—and consulted a labor lawyer.

Kathy's lawyer advised her to change her sales proposal, addressing the potential situation head-on. Now, among other things, Kathy's standard proposal terms specify that the customer must pay a specific hiring fee should it spirit an employee away from her. Kathy wisely has clients sign off on all sales proposals before she begins a project.

This is good practice. When addressing hiring fees in your proposal, you can specify either a fixed amount or a percentage of the affected employee's salary—whatever works for you. Then, should the unthinkable happen, you have the option of charging that hiring fee. You can also choose to reduce or disregard it, depending on your future business expectations with that client. In the meantime, you're better protected and you've lessened the blow of losing an employee.

How to Stop Runaway Legal and Accounting Expenses

It is very difficult to control service expenses that are billed by the hour, specifically attorney and accountant fees. Knowing your firm's hourly rate isn't the same as knowing your total end costs. Often, you don't even have a good sense of what an hour will buy you.

Runaway costs are like a runaway train—an accident waiting to happen. As a result, ever-vigilant PRO members have developed various strategies for reining in legal and accounting costs. These include:

- Ask your firm for a fixed cost for a given project. You can ask, can't you? At the very least, insist on an estimate.

- If the firm won't provide you with a fixed cost, try to negotiate a cap. To encourage the firm to come in under the cap, offer to share the cost difference. In other words, offer an efficiency bonus.

- Break big projects down into smaller segments, and place a cap on each individual segment. Specify that cost approval is necessary for fees that exceed any of the caps. This ensures that you will avoid unpleasant surprises at the completion of a big project.

- To get a growing sense of what your service firm's hour buys you, review bills closely as they come in. What kind of work gets done in an hour's time?

- Occasionally request competitive bids from other firms. This allows you to see if your service firm is operating efficiently—that you're receiving good value, hour by hour.

- Consider a yearly retainer. Some law firms will work on a retained basis, excluding litigation fees. If you call on your firm's services frequently throughout the year, this could be a good deal for you.

- Don't accept runaway service fees. It's up to you to step on the brake!

A Baker's Dozen: Ideas for Outsmarting a Soft Economy

Have you decided not to play the recession game? Then take the offensive—and make some of these moves part of your game plan. Not all of them will work for you, but they can spur new ideas that will lead you to action.

1. *Upgrade Your Personnel.* Now's the time to enhance your number one asset. People make a difference. Review your staff. Identify who actively contributes to your company's performance, creativity, and future direction. Don't be satisfied with the status quo; now is the time to raise the performance bar. A few years ago, it may have been difficult to find talented candidates. You may have settled for hires with less-than-optimum skills. Ask yourself, *Would I hire these people now, knowing their strengths and weaknesses? Do their strengths complement their job requirements?* If not, now is the ideal opportunity to look for people who can make a true difference.

2. *Review Compensation and Benefit Programs.* In most small companies (especially service businesses) employee compensation is the single largest expense. Review your compensation policies. Are they tied to performance? If not, consider changing your compensation structure. Is it possible to lower base salaries while increasing results-driven bonuses—and not just in sales, but throughout the organization? Many small

businesses do not measure performance, working by subjective standards rather than objective measurements. The problem? You cannot incent performance unless you can measure it. An employee won't know if he or she is doing a good job unless there is a standard.

Fringe benefits make up an important part of the compensation package. In general, fringe benefits equate to 30 to 45 percent of employee wages. Health insurance is increasing by 25 to 40 percent each year. Consider cost-saving plans such as Medical Savings Accounts (MSAs), cafeteria programs, and greater cost sharing with employees.

3. *Maximize Vendor Concessions.* When the economy is soft, it's a good time to negotiate with vendors. The terms are limited only by your imagination. For example:

- *Renegotiate your rent.* If your lease will expire in the next few years, consider a longer-term lease with concessions as a trade off. Negotiate an immediate rent reduction in exchange for a new, longer-term lease.

- *Enter into long-term supply contracts with vendors.* Lock in forward pricing and hedge future costs. Often, price and payment terms may be renegotiated. If you have cash and can pay promptly, you can enjoy price discounts, promotion allowances, restocking or obsolescence charges, catalog allowances, and other advantages.

- *Renegotiate terms such as extended payment, consignment inventory, vendor housing of inventory, etc. if you're not rich in cash.* Sell your vendors on the premise that by working with you, they'll do more business. Discuss promotional allowances, product placement positioning, catalog allowances, and co-op advertising. These strategies will help you sell more product/services—and use more of their product/services.

4. *Upgrade and Enhance Processes.* Improving processes should be an ongoing activity. In soft markets, it is even more important to squeeze costs out of your system. Many companies have used TQM or variations thereof to achieve improvements. If you have not yet tried a formal approach, now's the time to investigate it.

5. *Refine Your Sales Strategy.* When business is soft, don't assume that the old way of working still works. Smart companies are constantly reinventing strategies to satisfy the demands of business, clients, market conditions, and the acceptance of their product/service.

   - Categorize your customers—not all of them are profitable. In all probability, you have reduced your staff; now look at your customer base. Put your assets where you can make a profit or have strong future potential.

   - It may be necessary to "fire" accounts or raise prices to unprofitable customers who consume resources. Focus your sales team on selling your most profitable product/service. Use gross profit as a measure—or better yet GMROI (Gross Margin Return on Investment), gross margin that considers inventory turns on products.

• Focus sales activity on accounts that produce the greatest results. In addition, be mindful of additional products/services you can market to specific customers.

6. *Increase "Throughput."* In a soft market, customers typically purchase in smaller quantities and contract for smaller projects. As a result, you must shorten lead times, set-up times, project preparation, etc. Look for ways to handle shorter runs and projects, or power up your "throughput," as we say in the manufacturing world. Challenge old concepts. Leadership means defying the status quo.

7. *Create Strategic Alliances.* Strategic alliances don't have to be sophisticated. You can reduce expenses with simple strategies such as buying pools, rent sharing, and equipment sharing. Make use of manufacturers' reps, brokers, and export agents to sell your products/services.

8. *Target Customers of Troubled Competitors.* Is a competitor in trouble? That company's customers make excellent prospects! Your competitor may not be able to provide the required service or quality or adequately maintain the customer/vendor relationship.

First identify which of your competitors may be struggling, then identify their key customers and initiate an active sales campaign to win them over. Many customers resist change until a distressing event occurs that prompts them to act. If your competitor's customers fear a supply disruption, that may be the catalyst you need to initiate a switch.

9. *Acquire Competitors.* A more aggressive strategy is to acquire the competition itself. This might mean the entire company, a division, product lines, equipment, etc. (A note of caution: all acquisitions must fulfill one your strategic goals.) In a soft economy, goals may include increasing market penetration and amortization of overhead, among other things. A soft economy may also create the opportunity of strategic acquisition that helps you meet your goals.

10. *Enhance Brand and Mind Share.* Many companies are cutting marketing activities to reduce expenses. Is this wise? No! Studies show that the companies maintaining or increasing marketing efforts during soft economies enjoy larger business increases once the economy firms. If you have the vision and the cash, increased marketing is a smart move. The objective is to increase "mind share," so customers think about you first when it's time to purchase your product or service. Marketing communication firms and publications are hungry for business now. This is a good time to undertake advertising or branding

programs, negotiating the most for your marketing dollars—in both the short term and the long term.

11. *Vertical Integration.* This may be the time to make the investment of reducing costs through vertical integration. Equipment and processes may cost less now and yield better amortization of overhead. A more aggressive strategy is to acquire a troubled vendor. It can not only give you a competitive edge, but shorten the learning curve to self-sufficiency.

12. *Review Cash Flow and P&L Activity.* Cash is king, especially during tough times. Make sure your lines of credit are adequate. Don't allow yourself to run short of working capital or you will spend all your time managing cash. If your company does not have financial controls, get them in place. You may need them to survive...and you definitely will need them to grow. Cash flow projectives are especially important. You may need to manage by cash and not your profit and loss statement.

Here are key financial controls to implement:
- Cash flow projections and statements
- Monthly revenue projections
- Monthly expense projections with variances
- Capital equipment budgets
- Inventory acquisition budgets and variances

This is also the time to sell obsolete equipment and inventory. Cash is king!

13. *Strengths and Weaknesses.* This is definitely the time to seriously review your company's strengths and weaknesses, if you haven't already done so. If you have any big weaknesses, remedy them now. In tough times, survivors hunker down and perform because there is no flow of resources for fixing chronic problems. Don't use Band-Aids; determine the root problem and fix it! At the same time, recognize your strengths and act to build on them. Tough times require focus and maximum return on effort, investment, money, and manpower.

When the going gets tough, the tough get going. These strategies are designed to spur you into action. Get off the recession bus and head for a brighter destination.

Turn Brown Into Green: How to Reduce Your Shipping Costs

Don't think you have any control over UPS shipping costs? Think again! There are creative solutions that reduce shipping expenses. Shipping consolidation is one such solution.

For example, Steven's Chicago-based parts company ships numerous packages to West Coast customers. Steven found that shipping between different UPS zones—from Midwest to West Coast—accounted for the bulk of his high shipping costs.

As a result, he began hiring overland trucks to carry his consolidated packages to a centralized West Coast delivery point. Once the packages were dropped off, they were individually shipped locally via UPS at a much more affordable intra-zone rate. By using a skip-zone strategy, Steven reduced his West Coast shipping costs.

Then Steven learned he could save more dramatically by using "dead-head" trucks for UPS consolidation and LTL (less than truckload) shipments. These trucks—based on the West Coast—make one-way deliveries to the Midwest, then return home empty. Already on the road, their operators were happy to have a shipment to deliver.

Steven found half-filled trucks offer additional options. Because his packages are small but heavy, he looks for trucks partially filled with bulky yet lightweight items. In other words, he helps fill the trucks while staying within the weight maximums. The truck operators make more money while Steven saves more money.

And guess what? Shrewd Steven didn't pass the savings onto his customers. His shipping fees—once a headache—now turn a profit for him!

Greener Pastures: Realize Savings While Relocating

Moving your plant or office? Relocating presents wonderful opportunities for reducing all kinds of expenses you might not consider. Whether buying or renting space, the key is to negotiate these expenses before you sign on the dotted line. Once you've committed, your leverage is lost.

You wouldn't pay sticker price for a car. Why pay sticker price for anything? Here are some of the expenses that relocating PRO members have successfully negotiated:

- *Real Estate Taxes*—Your company will be pumping money into the local economy and that has value. Find out what the city or county will offer you to make their home your own.
- *Utilities*—If you're going to be a big user of gas, water, or electrical utilities, you may qualify for a discount. And even if you're not a big user, you might get a discount simply by asking.
- *Employee Testing and Training*—Will you be providing job opportunities to local residents? Your new community may offer you a stipend to offset testing and training costs.
- *Renting Office Space*—See if your landlord is willing to throw in some built-ins to sweeten the deal, saving you construction costs. Similarly, now's the time to negotiate CAM costs—costs for common area maintenance. These costs rise over time; setting caps in your leasing agreement will save you money, now and later.
- *Free Rent*—See if your landlord will offer you several months of free rent as a welcome present.

Whatever your reason for relocating, your move offers you some unique savings opportunities. Take advantage of them!

Seminar Amnesia: Hold Employees Accountable for What They Learn

Sending your employees to training seminars is a great way to encourage professional growth, boost morale, and create loyalty. It benefits the company by introducing fresh thinking. But it also represents an investment for you. You want to make sure that you get your money's worth—that your employees actually use the knowledge they learn.

Typically, an employee returns from a seminar bursting with new ideas and inspiration. Within minutes, however, he is jolted back into the reality of the everyday—returning phone calls, cleaning out his in-box, and tackling the backlog of problems that piled up in his absence. Diving back into the bustle of day-to-day work, he quickly forgets all that he learned while away. It's something we've all done at one time or another.

PRO members have dubbed this "seminar amnesia." One group came up with a viable solution. It's worked for them—it may work for you. Here's how you use it: encourage employees to attend meaningful seminars, provided that they agree to be held accountable for what they learn. As soon as an employee returns from a seminar, he or she must report to you, providing a verbal synopsis of what they learned. More important, they must be prepared to apply it to their work—and that means telling you what he or she will accomplish within the next thirty days as a result of their new knowledge.

Thirty days later, you meet again. Your employee reports to you what he or she has achieved. Now you have something you can measure. Now you have a cure for seminar amnesia.

Conducting SWOT Analysis

Are you familiar with SWOT analysis? If not, you should be. SWOT is an essential component of the strategic planning process. In a nutshell, SWOT represents a study of your company's:

- S—Strengths
- W—Weaknesses
- O—Opportunities
- T—Threats

Once you've identified these factors in detail, you're in a better position to formulate short- and long-term goals, the basis of strategic planning. And because the world—and your organization—is constantly changing, a SWOT analysis should be conducted periodically, perhaps every other year.

An examination of your strengths and weaknesses is internal in nature, while the assessment of opportunities and threats is focused on the external universe. Let's look at each category individually:

- *Strengths*—Your company's strengths are those things your organization does well, those characteristics you ought to build on. Often these are the very qualities that differentiate you from your competition. However, be aware that your strengths can easily become weaknesses, should you lose them. For example, if your key strength is your high-powered sales force and your best salespeople are lured away, your former strength is now your Achilles' heel. (Therefore, your strategic plan should include ways to reinforce your corporate strengths—say, by sweetening compensation or diversifying your sales force.)

- *Weaknesses*—You're probably aware of some areas of vulnerability, but conducting a SWOT analysis forces you to face them head-on. And sometimes you'll be taken completely by surprise. Either way, once major weaknesses are identified, fixing them—thoroughly and permanently—should be your first priority. A house cannot stand on a faulty foundation.

- *Opportunities*—Evaluating opportunities means taking a good look at the world around you. Pending legislation, market trends, forces of nature, the economy—all of these represent potential opportunities. Being the first in your industry to identify them gives you a competitive edge.

- *Threats*—Threats are the flip side of opportunities. All the factors mentioned above—legislation, market trends, acts of God, the economy—can work for or against you. For example, Congress passes a law mandating the use of a particular product—say, a certain type of children's car seat. If you happen to manufacture those car seats, that represents a rich opportunity. But what if Congress later repeals that law? Your opportunity has turned on you and now threatens your company's future.

The knowledge of potential opportunities and threats is extremely valuable—and should be the starting point of your contingency planning.

SWOT analysis provides you with a snapshot of your company's health, but that's not all. It offers an important secondary benefit: ensuring that all members of management are on the same page. SWOT analysis is a structured way to build consensus and agreement—a key ingredient to successful strategic planning.

Faux Searches—A Competitive Tool

Want to know how another company gets something done? A faux search—employee search, that is—is one way to find out. Some PRO members have enjoyed great success with this technique.

First, identify what information you're looking for and where it is maintained (who has it?). Then, contact those potential candidates who are likely to have it and conduct potential job interviews.

You can do this directly, but you're more likely to strike gold if you hire a third party—yes, a recruiter—to conduct the search on your behalf. Chances are your recruiter has received such requests before. Once you have your candidates, conduct actual job interviews. Who knows, you may even get a great new hire out of the process.

Your first objective, however, is to collect information. As with any interview, ask the key questions: What are your responsibilities? What have you accomplished?

What process do you use? How did this process come about? What role did you play in creating it?

Sound too much like industrial espionage for your comfort? Consider this: it's each company's responsibility to tell employees what information is confidential. In all probability, you will not expose any trade secrets or illuminating discoveries. More than likely you will pick up a few good details that allow you to tweak your own processes.

If you want to keep succeeding, never stop learning. The faux search just offers you one more tool for mining new knowledge.

Making Commitments or How to Eat an Elephant

How do you eat an elephant? One bite at a time, of course! It's a corny old joke, but when it comes to tackling major projects, it's an exquisite metaphor. From high school term papers to high-level reorganizations, we often find ourselves paralyzed in the face of enormous projects. Getting started is the hardest part.

PRO members disagree on many points, but there's one thing we all agree on: the only way to accomplish a project of elephantine proportions is to break it down into bite-size portions. So divide your project into manageable mouthfuls and schedule each "meal" by setting deadlines. This helps you formulate a plan and determine what resources you'll need at every stage (does this call for a butter knife or a meat cleaver?). This process also creates the opportunity for intermediate goal setting, so you can measure your progress along the way.

PERT diagrams, Gant charts, backwards calendars—these techniques, all used in formalized project planning—are simply variations on this theme. How do you eat an elephant? One bite at a time.

In summary, the transformation from entrepreneur to leader doesn't happen overnight. Often, the metamorphosis is gradual and intuitive. But it is absolutely necessary, because a company can't go anywhere without someone to point the way.

CHAPTER TWO

SALES

Sales are the lifeblood of every organization. No company can survive without them. Yet in all too many small businesses, there is no real methodology in place. The sales "process," to phrase it loosely, is a patchwork of familiar routines that everyone hopes will work.

But hoping and wishing won't make it so. Selling isn't magic; it's a science. To approach it scientifically, you should identify what works for your business, document it, and create your own defined, repeatable process. Here's how.

YOUR UNIQUE SELLING PROPOSITION

The first step is to determine what sets your company apart. What special benefits do you offer? What makes your company unique?

Do You Know Your USP?

Every company should have a USP—a Unique Selling Proposition.

A USP is the specific benefit your customers get from your product or service. It is a benefit offered exclusively by your company—your competition cannot or does not offer it. Declaring your USP is essentially creating your brand. It's what differentiates you from everyone else.

Now don't get nervous, because PRO members are about to share a big secret. Your USP does not need to be truly unique. What makes it unique is that you are the first to claim it. And once you do, no one else will.

Years ago, I was in the hand tool manufacturing business. We drew on our chrome-plating process to create our USP. The truth was that our chrome-plating process was no different than anyone else's. But by highlighting this step, we gave the impression that our process was superior and therefore our product was superior, too.

Do you have a USP? If not, it's time to create one.

Crafting Your 30-Second Introduction

Your mother was right; you only get one chance to make a first impression. Studies indicate that people make up their minds about someone within one minute of meeting them. Every second does count—that's why you need a powerful 30-second introduction.

Whether you're formally networking or casually chatting in an elevator, you'll find plenty of opportunities to use your 30-second "commercial." And if you ever attend professional meetings where you're asked to introduce yourself, it's an absolute must.

The best 30-second introductions stand out, usually by beginning with an attention-getting comment. They're sometimes funny, always memorable, and they inspire people to want to know more.

For example, as the founder of PRO, I create and facilitate peer group advisory boards. Is that how I begin my 30-second introduction? Never! Depending on the audience and circumstance, I use one of the following:

"I create business fertilizer. I help companies nourish and grow…"

or

"I am a business chiropractor. I help straighten companies out…"

Here's another good example: PRO member Harry owns a company that distributes janitorial supplies—not the most glamorous or riveting industry. But when Harry begins his 30-second introduction, he immediately draws the attention of everyone in the room, simply by announcing:

"I talk dirty!"

In three little words, Harry has broken the ice, created a conversational starting point, and made sure he will be remembered.

Once you have an attention-getting opener, follow up by explaining the benefit you have to offer. (Look back at my first example. The opening statement, *"I sell business fertilizer,"* is explained by the second benefit-rich sentence, *"I help companies nourish and grow."*)

Complete your introduction by stating who you are and what your company does. Conclude by restating the problem you solve for your customer. For example:

"I sell business fertilizer. I help companies nourish and grow. My name is Ray Silverstein, and I own a company named PRO. PRO facilitates peer group advisory boards for small business owners. We enable entrepreneurs to share ideas and insights and function as one another's board of directors, so they don't feel alone at the top."

THE SALES FUNNEL

If sales are a science, the sales process—a defined, repeatable sequence of activities—can be expressed as a mathematical model. We call this the "sales funnel." Once you create your company's sales funnel, you have a blueprint for repeating your successful sales formula, plus a yardstick for measuring your salespeople's performance.

Defining Your Sales Funnel

Whether you know it or not, your operation has its own distinct sales funnel—the telescoping start-to-finish process you use to make sales happen.

You begin the process by casting a wide net for prospective new customers. Gradually, through a series of defined activities, you narrow your scope to a defined number of buying customers.

For example, an insurance agent might start with a broad direct marketing program, such as telemarketing or direct mail, to reach thousands of potential customers.

As a result of the direct marketing effort, a percentage of interested prospects will be identified. The agent will arrange appointments with each one of them.

A percentage of these appointments will be kept and then a percentage of those kept will result in the agent's opportunity to prepare a proposal. He will ultimately present a number of those proposals to his prospects. Then a percentage of those presentations will result in a final sale.

Your sales funnel, of course, is unique to your organization. But you do have one. And once you've identified it, you can mathematically define the percentage of response typically occurring at each tier of the funnel.

What is the benefit? Once you look at the results, you can identify your weak points and improve them accordingly. You can tweak your sales process to improve your end results.

Finally, you can measure the performance of your sales staff against the standard. If your closing standard is 8 percent, but your newest salesperson is performing at 4 percent, you now know you need to work on his closing skills.

Knowing your sales funnel is a valuable tool that helps you define your processes, measure your people, and identify areas where training is needed.

The Sales Funnel

Direct Marketing Campaign

Prospects Identified

Appointments Set

Appointments Kept

Proposal Prepared

Proposal Presented

Sale!

What's the Best Way to Compensate Salespeople?

The subject of sales compensation comes up frequently at PRO meetings. There are many ways to compensate salespeople—e.g., salary, commission, a draw, or some combination of salary and commission. Each method has its pros and cons. The method you choose should depend on the type of salespeople you want to attract, the product you sell, and the length of your sales cycle.

In general, if you pay your salespeople 100 percent commission, you will attract aggressive, entrepreneurial, independent spirits. If you pay a large base salary, you will attract quieter, more security-minded workers (who may not be as aggressive, but they might excel at relationship building).

Now consider this: if your compensation formula depends heavily upon commissions, your salespeople are more likely to feel the accounts belong to them—not to you. This frees them to believe it is easy to leave your company and take "their" accounts with them. On the other hand, a salesperson who receives a large base salary will not feel as proprietary about his or her accounts—a key advantage of the generous base salary.

Many PRO members started out by paying new sales-people a draw against future commissions. However, they often found that draws have a drawback. What happens when a salesperson never starts selling? A large negative draw accumulates. Eventually, convinced he will never be able to pay back what in essence has become a salary, the salesperson will leave when the draw is reduced or elimi-nated. At that point, the employer loses the salesperson, the amount of his draw, and the time invested in his training.

PRO members have found that, if they choose to use a draw system, it should be a declining draw. In other words, the amount of the draw should decrease over time, as the employee is gradually expected to sell. For example, decrease the draw at sixty days, again at ninety days, and perhaps eliminate it altogether after 120 days of employment. The length of the draw and the reduction schedule should be balanced against the length of your sales cycle. In particular, care has to be taken when the sales cycle is long.

What about those long sales cycles? Most managers like to measure sales performance on billing achievement, which is impossible in the early stages of a long sales cycle. In such cases, it makes more sense to measure a new salesperson's activity—the number of calls and pro-posals they generate, how often they follow up, etc.

Once you've identified your sales funnel, you know which activities will lead to success. By measuring actual activity against the funnel, you can measure performance.

This also works with salespeople who collect large base salaries. The sales funnel allows you to create meas-urable goals for specific activities (e.g., fifteen sales calls a month). Your salesperson knows that achieving his goals will allow him to keep his job and salary.

What's the ideal balance of salary and commissions? Commissions motivate salespeople to sell; salaries bind them to your company. Studies by sales compensation consultants suggest that setting salary at 40 percent of expected earnings could be the optimum formula. Of course, any formula must be tailored to your company, salespeople, product, and sales cycle.

Whatever formula you use, make sure it's simple and easy to understand. A complex incentive formula is in itself a disincentive.

EXPANDING THE SALES FORCE

As we discussed earlier, you can't do everything yourself. You have to learn to delegate! It's not an easy thing to do, particularly when it comes to all-important sales. But in order to grow, you have to leverage up on your salespeo-ple. Here's how to take it one step at a time.

When You're the Rainmaker

If you're like most entrepreneurs, you're probably your company's original rainmaker.

Rainmakers are highly competitive, assertive, optimistic, and have a strong desire to win. In other words, you are your company's most effective salesperson. Yes, there are small businesses started by people with strong technical abilities, but the ones that really grow are those driven by a strong sense of salesmanship.

So what's the problem with that? Sooner or later, a company founded by a rainmaker will run into problems. The problem is time saturation. How can you handle increasing administrative and/or management responsibilities when you are also responsible for your company's sales activity? How can your company grow when its primary sales achiever is too busy to nurture that growth?

This question comes up frequently in PRO meetings. PRO members have experimented with various solutions. (Regardless of how you do it, it's a crucial bridge you must cross if you want to grow from a start-up to a managed company.) Here are some PRO members' solutions:

- *Solution #1—Good:* Hire an administrative assistant, like Vera did. Vera is a first-class rainmaker— an activity she didn't want to give up. So Vera hired an administrative assistant to take over many of her day-to-day activities and to provide inside sales support. It appears to be working for Vera now. But the solution is only temporary, because the company is still entirely dependent on Vera for its sales growth, health, and value. Eventually, Vera will need to find another solution.

- *Solution #2—Better:* Hire salespeople, like John did. The problem is that John wanted another rainmaker just like himself; and rainmakers (or "finders") are tough to find. Eventually, John realized it was much easier to hire "minders"—people who can ably service the business and slowly grow the accounts. The type of people you hire should be determined by your goals and your product. (You can learn more about finders, minders, and grinders in the section that follows.)

- *Solution #3—Best:* Create a sales organization, like Mike did. Mike took the time to define his company's sales process. In other words, he charted the sales funnel we talked about earlier. Because he has defined his company's sales process, he can measure and manage the performance of both individual salespeople and his entire sales organization. This is indeed the best long-term solution.

Rainmaking is a gift. However, in order to foster your company's growth, you need to do more—you need to lead. And that means quantifying your rainmaking process so others can repeat it. It means defining your sales funnel and building an entire sales organization. Ultimately, the value of a business is greatly increased if the daily activity is not based on you—the rainmaker—but on an entire team.

High-Powered Hiring: Finders, Minders, and Grinders

A successful salesperson is worth his weight in gold. One of the toughest challenges is finding the right person for that very important sales function.

When evaluating salespeople, you might study a candidate's experience, track record, and industry contacts. But no matter how carefully you analyze the criteria, sales hiring often remains hit-or-miss. Many PRO discussions have revolved around this hiring conundrum.

One of the revelations to emerge from PRO meetings is the idea of hiring people by sales "type" or personality—by matching the right type of person to the job. We have identified three distinct sales personalities:

- *The Finder*—The finder loves the thrill of the hunt. He or she is an aggressive go-getter, the classic rainmaker. As soon as a sale is clinched, he is off on the trail of his next quarry. The finder is the one you want when you're seeking new accounts. Typically, the finder is terrific on the road, but may have few allies in-house. He tends to be arrogant and leaves service and follow-through to others.

- *The Minder*—The minder is a relationship builder. She or he is a people person and a problem solver. Their goal is not the conquest of the sale, but forging mutually beneficial long-term relationships. The minder is committed to client satisfaction and considers ongoing service part of the sale. If acquiring add-on business from existing clients is a large part of your operation, the minder is the one for you. She will not generate the exciting production numbers of the finder, but her persistency ratios tend to be high.

- *The Grinder*—The grinder is a relentless plodder. Rejection won't stop him. Repetition doesn't bother him. While the grinder has neither the finder's flair nor the minder's service standards, he is the ideal candidate for high-volume sales calls, such as door-to-door sales.

Now that you know the three sales personalities, your job is to determine which one is right for your particular sales position. Consider the products or services you sell and the way they are sold. Review your sales successes; what approaches work best with your clients? Think also about your company and its organization. It won't take you long to determine which personality type is right for the job.

For many organizations, the best solution is actually a combination of sales personalities that complement one another's strengths. For example, the finder—an outside salesperson—brings in a new account. Then he turns it over to the minder—perhaps an inside salesperson—to solidify the relationship by providing attention and service.

REFERRALS

The referral is a very powerful sales tool, yet many sales organizations fail to utilize it. If your salespeople aren't asking satisfied customers for referrals, you are missing a huge opportunity to grow your business. The hardest part is just getting started.

How to Get and Use Referrals

How do you get referrals? By asking for them. How do you ask for them? You begin by expanding your thinking. Every business relationship you create has the potential to lead you to other relationships. If a customer buys from you and is happy with the product/service he or she receives, why wouldn't you ask for that customer's referrals?

Buyers prefer not to buy cold. Referrals create a comfort level that eases the sales process. A service business is a particularly hard sell; prospective buyers understand what good service is, but they can't hold it in their hands or watch it work before they buy. Therefore, the testimonial of someone they know goes a long way towards making a sale.

How can you get in the habit of cultivating referrals? Here are some key steps:

1. *Go Prospecting for Referrals.* You can ask anyone for a referral: a customer, a contact, even a prospect. When's the best time to ask for a referral? Any time! For example, when you first begin working with a new customer, make referrals part of your front-end agreement. In other words, get your new customer to agree to provide you with four or five referrals once you've proven yourself. Do a great job, and then go back and collect those referrals.

In addition, anytime a customer says something positive about you or your company, follow up with a thank-you and a request for referrals. In addition, get in the habit of periodically asking customers for referrals.

Planting the seed that you are building your business on referrals is not a negative; it's a positive. After all, you can only get referrals when people are satisfied with your work. When you first meet a prospect, let them know you place great value in referrals and that you earn them by providing high-quality products and services.

2. *Exceed Your Customers' Expectations.* If you can get your customer to acknowledge that you've done a great job, you're halfway there. But to exceed customer expectations, you must know what those expectations are. Find out what "great service" means to them. Ask them why they do business with your company. Periodically ask them how you're doing, informally and through satisfaction surveys. And by all means, encourage them to complain! Complaints, no matter how small, give you the opportunity to solve a problem and be a hero, while obtaining valuable insights for improving service.

3. *Form Referral Alliances.* Form relationships with others who can provide you with referrals—and who you can also provide referrals to. In other words, build a network of mutually supportive contacts. *Then work that network!* This means not only providing your contacts with referrals, but helping them solve problems and being a good listener.

Make sure your contacts know what a good prospect looks like to you. You don't want cool leads; you want hot, enthusiastic referrals! This means investing in and nurturing relationships with your contacts.

Find ways to stay in touch and offer support; it pays off. Be a valuable resource.

    4. *Be Prepared at Networking Events.* When you have a networking opportunity, be prepared to answer questions such as "How are you?" or "What's new?" Be ready to talk about a new source you've found, an exciting new client, or some other success. Be enthusiastic. Ironically, the best answers are those that sound entirely spontaneous.

In addition, create goals for each event you attend. For example:

- Plan to speak meaningfully with at least three new people.
- Make a point of meeting the speaker and engaging him or her in conversation.
- Introduce at least two people to each other.
- Identify what information you'd like to learn.
- If you meet someone you'd like to connect with, ask permission to call him or her for an appointment. Try to schedule a date to call.

Don't allow yourself to be lazy and stick with the same old crowd. Setting goals such as these forces you make the most of networking events.

By all means, go after referrals as a way to grow your business. And don't just go after bland, ordinary referrals—turn up the heat to make them work harder for you.

CASE STUDY: LYLE

PRO member Lyle has built his entire business on referrals. How did he get so good at it?

Years ago, when Lyle was starting out as a young salesman, he was lucky to be trained by a very savvy sales manager. When Lyle was in training, the manager accompanied him on his sales calls.

Eager to stay on schedule, Lyle frequently consulted his watch. Observing Lyle's habit, the manager advised him to stick a red dot on his watch. Every time he saw that dot, his manager told him, it was time to ask for a customer referral.

The result? Lyle quickly got into the habit of requesting referrals. Not surprisingly, all of Lyle's salespeople now wear red dots on their watches.

Turn Up the Heat: How to Cook Up Hot Referrals

Not all leads are created equal. PRO members recognize four levels of leads:

- *Level 1*—You've been given a name and phone number, but you can't use your referral source's name. This is the equivalent of a well-targeted cold call.
- *Level 2*—You not only have a name and phone number, you have permission to use your referral source's name. You're getting warmer.
- *Level 3*—You have all of the above, plus some

information about your prospect. This is a truly warm referral.

- *Level 4*—You have all of the above—plus the knowledge that your prospect has a specific need for your product or service. Now you're hot, hot, hot!

No matter what level you start at with a given lead, try to bump it up a level.

For example, to move from Level 2 to Level 3, ask your source questions like these:

- How do you know this person? How would you define your relationship?
- What is his/her exact title and responsibilities?
- What type of personality is he/she—i.e., direct, standoffish, etc.?
- What can you tell me about his/her business?
- Do you think we'll get along? Do we have any common interests?

And to move from Level 3 to Level 4, ask:

- What are some of the challenges this person is facing (either in general or related to my product/service)?

Once you learn that your prospect has a need for your services, ask your source for advice on how to proceed—e.g., "Can I bring this up with Mary directly, or should I be more subtle?"

Here are some other ways to heat up your referrals:

- Ask your source to write a note on your brochure or business card.
- Ask your source to phone your prospect and tell him/her about you.

- Ask your source to write an email to the same effect.
- Invite both the source and the prospect to breakfast or lunch.
- A good source is a treasure. Treat him or her well. Always thank your source for referrals, and keep him/her posted regarding your progress.

Sales do not occur by magical phenomenon. The only way to ensure ongoing success is to approach your sales activities scientifically, using every tool at your disposal. Like a scientist, note what works for you and what doesn't. Then create your own defined sales process. When you control the process, you also control the outcome.

CHAPTER THREE

SALES MANAGEMENT

Since sales are essential to a company's survival, sales management should be undertaken very seriously. Yet some small businesses unwittingly set their salespeople up for certain failure! They make the wrong hiring choices, provide inadequate training, and then fail to measure performance. They distract their sales force with false priorities. Consider this a primer on the care and feeding of one of your most valuable resources: your salespeople.

SALES MANAGEMENT RESPONSIBILITIES

As sales manager, you are responsible for ensuring that your salespeople succeed. How can you possibly do that? First, by hiring the right people. Then by giving them the tools and training they need, starting with an understanding of your sales funnel.

The Gestation Period of a New Salesperson

It's a puzzle, all right: how long do you give new salespeople to prove they have what it takes?

A new, not-yet-performing salesperson is a large expense, both in terms of dollars (salary, draw, travel and entertainment costs) and opportunity cost (the sales that are lost if they fail to produce).

When breaking in new salespeople, the objective is to recognize signs of potential failure as early as possible. How do you do this? By measuring their activity, right from the first week. Are they taking the specific actions necessary for sales success? Are they making the required number of phone calls and cold calls? Getting the necessary number of appointments? Submitting enough proposals? Once you know your sales funnel, you know exactly what actions they should be performing.

If a new salesperson isn't performing the right tasks from the beginning, chances are that he or she will never perform up to par. If someone is taking the right steps but isn't getting results, that person probably needs more training. (The other possibility is that his or her sales personality doesn't fit with your type of product or service.)

Hiring successful salespeople is difficult. Your best chance for success is to determine early on if a salesperson isn't going to work for you. If a change is required, take it soon, before you've made a large investment.

In that unhappy event, your only recourse is to cut him or her loose and try again. Don't give up on finding the right person. If you've made a mistake, study it and learn from it. Ask yourself: Why didn't it work out the first time? Why was that person wrong for the job? What attributes does the right candidate need? How can I make a better hire next time? Study your successes.

How Do You Train a Salesperson?

The first step is to hire the right person, as previously discussed. As one PRO member tells his new salespeople, "I can't give you what your mother didn't give you!" If someone doesn't have the right personality, no amount of training will make him a star.

Assuming you hired wisely, how do you go about training? Many small companies make the mistake of having trainees study the product catalog, hang around the office, and then hit the road. This is rather like teaching your kids to swim by throwing them into the deep end of a pool to see if they'll float.

Successful, sales-driven companies have a proven sales presentation that works for them. New salespeople are thoroughly taught how to give this presentation and answer anticipated objectives. They rehearse and rehearse until the presentation is second nature. Only then are they sent out in the great wide world.

Trainees should first accompany experienced salespeople on calls, so they can observe and learn. Eventually, the trainees should begin presenting while the veteran salesperson observes. This way, the experienced salesperson can offer support and also critique the beginner's performance.

Don't have someone in-house to train your trainee? Hire an outside sales trainer to provide the selling skills your trainee will need. Meanwhile, be sure you are providing the product knowledge and market understanding he or she is going to need. Don't send trainees out into the field until you are 100 percent sure they are ready. Remember, they are representing you! Don't program them for failure.

And don't assume that some initial success means you've got a winner. Periodically accompany your salespeople on calls to make sure they are not taking shortcuts with your presentation or developing bad habits.

In addition, don't assume that someone who is personable or has sales experience automatically knows how to sell your product. The seller's personality must complement your product or service. Selling is an artful science. It takes the right person and the right training.

RECRUITMENT

They say you can't make a silk purse out of a sow's ear. The same goes for salespeople. You need to start with the right ingredients. How do you know what those ingredients are? Begin by creating a successful sales profile, then find people who have the right stuff.

Creating a Successful Sales Profile

As previously discussed, choosing the person with the right personality profile is the key to a successful hire. But how do you know what the right personality profile is for your organization?

The answer is easy: study your winners. What makes them tick? What traits do they have that makes them great performers? We're talking about personality traits, not learned behaviors.

Can you train someone to be a good salesperson? No. You can train him to perform certain activities that will make him a better salesperson, but not a good one. For example, you can't train someone to be intuitive or aggressive or detail oriented. You can't train someone to be a quick thinker or a problem solver or to handle rejection well.

So study your winners and identify their winning traits. For starters, use the finder/minder/grinder categories previously discussed. Then develop strategies that allow you to spot those traits during the interview process. Test your candidates in a way they might be tested on the job, and observe their reactions. Be willing to scratch the surface. Identify the personality profile that's right for your company, and you're halfway to finding the right person for the job.

CASE STUDY: CLARENCE

Clarence owns a high-end promotion business. He has one very successful saleswoman, Roz. Obviously, he wants more salespeople just like her.

Clarence has hired experienced salespeople with fabulous backgrounds and impressive resumes, but none have achieved the same results as Roz (who started out as a marketing assistant).

After studying Roz, Clarence realized she has a gift for communicating and empathizing with customers. Roz, who usually deals with product managers, understands their challenges and has a knack for suggesting creative solutions to their problems.

For Clarence, the ideal salesperson doesn't need extensive industry experience. What he or she does need is empathy, creativity, and good communication skills.

Where to Find Your Next Salesperson

Once you have your personality profile in your pocket, you can begin to keep your eyes open for people who fit the bill. This is a year-round activity, whether you currently need someone or not.

Where do you find good candidates? At PRO, experience has led us to develop a hierarchy for finding successful hires. Starting at the top, that hierarchy is:

1. People you already know.

2. People you trust who can make valid referrals.

3. Professional recruiters.

4. Classified ads and Internet recruitment sites.

Obviously, the best candidates are people you know or know of, whether through business or social activities. You already have a sense of who they are, although of course they still will need to prove their skills.

Looking for good people is like stocking a baseball club—you always want a bench of Triple-A players to bring up to the majors when needed. So when you come across someone who's got the right stuff (i.e., someone who fits your personality profile) get his or her contact information and keep it on file. Find reasons to keep in touch with them. That way, you'll be able to locate them when you have a job to offer them.

Many PRO members have had good experiences recruiting from outside their field. Yes, these candidates have to be trained, but on the plus side, they do not have preconceived notions of the business. Nor do they have bad habits that require retraining. When it comes to hiring, it pays to keep your eyes and your mind open.

What Do You Do When You Can't Find the Right Salesperson?

If you absolutely can't find a salesperson that meets all your requirements, perhaps you are requiring too much. In that event, you need to revise your sales model.

For example, PRO member John runs a roofing company. In the early days of his company, John made every sales call, returned to measure/quote each job, and then supervised each project. Like many business owners, John is something of a Renaissance man. Needless to say, sales took off.

Now John's company is too large for his hands-on involvement. Yet John wanted to continue providing his customers with a single point of contact, so he searched for a salesperson who could handle all the various aspects of the job.

The problem is, John has tried hiring several individuals, and not one of them has been able to handle the whole job. One sold exceptionally well, but was a poor estimator and a terrible supervisor. Another excelled at project supervision, but couldn't sell.

You get the picture. Each task required distinct skill sets, and John couldn't find one person who embodied them all. He could not find someone to replace himself.

At the urging of his fellow PRO members, John revamped his sales model. Now he has a rainmaker to capture sales, an estimator to measure the job and calculate the quotes, and a site supervisor to manage the jobs. If you can't find the right person, perhaps it's not your candidates—it's the job description.

SALES PRIORITIES

Small businesses, by definition, operate with limited resources. To get the most from your salespeople's time and energies, you have to set priorities. Not every customer is worth catering to.

Classifying Customers: You Can't Sell to Everyone

One of the key ingredients of formal strategic planning is defining your customer. This is very important when you own a small business. You simply don't have the resources, time, personnel, or capital to sell to everyone.

Lack of focus is a problem that often comes up at PRO meetings. Companies often try to be too many things to too many customers, thereby missing the chance to target their best potential customer. Ask yourself: Who is most likely to buy your product or service? What are their characteristics? What are your capabilities to supply them?

In sales and marketing, the key is to hunt with a rifle, not a shotgun. Precision pays off. Many companies take a scattershot approach, insisting that "everyone" is their potential customer. This may sound like big thinking, but it is in fact a big mistake. Let's switch metaphors. You only have a certain number of seeds in your seed bag. Sow them where they're most likely to produce a big harvest.

This philosophy applies not only to new customer sales, but to the servicing of your current customers. It's not wise to provide equal service to all customers, because not all customers are of equal value to you. Classify your customers—and reserve your very best priority service to the customers on your "A" list.

How do you classify your current customers? Determine what criteria are important to your company. It might be sales potential, profitability, payment history, ease of doing business, or perhaps some combination of these.

Ironically, many companies provide their best service to their worst customers! The squeaky wheel, after all, is the one that gets the grease. Chances are that the companies that hassle you the most (those on your "F" list) are getting your "A" level service. What's wrong with this picture?

There is both a direct and an indirect cost to servicing a customer, and you should assess both of them. Accounts that pay late, require maximum handholding, and have little or no profitability represent an opportunity cost. Why miss out on "A" level service opportunities at the expense of a problematic "F" level customer?

When and How to Fire a Customer

Most small business owners would never think of firing a customer. The very thought terrifies them; it goes against the entrepreneurial spirit.

But the truth is if you have a customer that is continually causing you problems (an "F" level customer), you need to be compensated for the hassle expense. And if the customer is unwilling to pay that cost, then in all probability you are better off without him. There is one very easy way to fire a customer: increase your prices. This is much less confrontational than telling someone you'll no longer do business with him. It then becomes the customer's choice. Either way, it's a win/win for you—you'll either be compensated for the hassle factor or you'll see the last of your problem customer.

Take the case of PRO member Mark, a building contractor who specializes in luxury homes. He recently turned down the opportunity to bid on a $2 million project. Why? Because he learned that his prospective customer had already fired his architect and another builder. From his contacts in the industry, he learned that this customer was impossible to satisfy. Although a $2 million project sounds tempting, Mark realized that this customer would place unreasonable demands on his time, money, and personnel. In the end, the cost outweighed the potential gain, so he walked away.

Firing customers goes hand-in-hand with classifying customers. Most small business owners don't consider the opportunities lost when they spend too much time servicing difficult customers. Yet these types of accounts devour both your internal and external resources.

Consider this: who is more important to you—your customers or your employees? Some employers insist that the customer comes first every time. But if you have problem customers who have your employees in a constant state of misery, then your employees are probably too stressed to service your good customers properly. In this scenario, you risk losing good customers—and good employees—at the expense of the bad ones.

Now don't go fire a customer just to prove you can do it. Rather, understand what kind of customer drives your business and creates profitability—and treat your customers accordingly.

MISCELLANEOUS IDEAS

You never know where that next good idea will come from. Here are some sales management techniques used in niche industries. Perhaps one of them will also work for you.

Improving Expectations with Customer Advisory Meetings

Want to strengthen your relationships with key customers to improve the quality of service you provide? One way to accomplish this goal is to invite select customers to an advisory meeting where you can learn how to better meet their needs.

A key ingredient of strategic planning today is asking customers what they want and need. You can't assume you know the answers or that you know what the market requires. Your customers can give you insights you never imagined, allowing you to serve them better. You can also use this opportunity to bounce ideas for new products and services off your best customers. At the same time, you'll give them a better sense of what they can expect from you. (Take pains to ensure it's a positive impression!)

PRO members have had excellent results with such advisory meetings. We recommend, however, that you follow these guidelines:

- Make sure your meeting is very well organized. Your customers' time is valuable; don't waste it.
- Limit the meeting from half a day to no more than

two days, depending on how much ground you want to cover.

- Pay your customers' expenses. The meeting doesn't have to be held at an extravagant resort, but it should be a professional, comfortable environment that encourages open discussion.
- Pick your attendees carefully, making sure they are not direct competitors. Make sure they represent different industries or geographical areas. And of course, limit invitations to your most important customers.
- To encourage your customers to attend, play to their egos. Tell them how important they are to your business. Tell them that you respect their knowledge and insights. Remind them that the objective is to better satisfy their needs. In our experience, most customers will attend.

You can also hold such a meeting with your outside sales agents. They are closer to the end consumer and have a better perspective on customer needs. They can also offer fresh insights regarding new products, levels of service, sales policies, etc.

Customer advisory meetings accomplish two goals at once: they strengthen your relationships and give you the knowledge you need to enhance your service.

How to Find Manufacturers' Reps

So you want to build your sales force by using manufacturers' reps, but you don't know where to find them?

They're out there! Here are some strategies PRO members use to find manufacturers' reps:

- *Contact trade associations.* If you're in a field that commonly uses reps, there is most likely a trade association of reps who work in your industry. If so, contact this association. It will be more than happy to provide you with a list of names.
- *Scout out industry trade shows.* Some companies attend trade shows specifically in order to make contact with reps. (It is entirely appropriate to hang a sign in your booth announcing that territories are available.)
- *Ask your top performers.* Already working with reps? Ask your top performers if they know qualified reps in other territories.
- *Ask your customers.* Ask your customers if they have a favorite rep, someone they would like to service their account. If a target customer suggests a specific rep organization, in all likelihood you will get additional business out of the account by using them.
- *Check a vendor's sign-in book.* Calling on a prospect or vendor? Sneak a peek at the sign-in book! You'll find all kinds of reps who are also calling on them. (This method works best when you do not have a strong relationship with the company you call on.)
- *Advertise in industry trade journals.* A rep organization is most likely to consider adding your company to the lines it already represents if:
1. You fill a void in its current representation of products/services.

2. It appears you will be a stronger supplier than the company it currently represents.

3. The organization is looking for new lines to represent.

When adding new reps, make sure they do not already represent your competition. A small competitive presence is acceptable, provided it is truly small and there is no substantial overlap or direct competition with the key products/services you want the reps to sell.

Is it preferable to choose a rep with a strong history of success and a good line of companies or a rep that is just starting out? It's a case-by-case decision. On the one hand, the established rep has the experience and contacts, but may already be under pressure from his existing companies to produce. He may not have the time to represent you well. On the other hand, a start-up rep may not have the strength to get into target companies or the skills to become an accomplished rep, but she may be hungry to prove herself and have more time to dedicate to you.

Once you find your manufacturers' reps, make sure you get the most out of them.

How to Get the Most from Manufacturers' Reps

Manufacturers' reps are generally a company's least expensive selling arm, but they are often the least effective one, too. Left unchecked, reps may be "inexpensive" only in the sense that you only pay commissions based on sales and collections. Motivation is the key to working with reps!

One PRO member views his reps the way a grocery store views its freezer case. There is only so much room in that case. The store manager can only add so much new merchandise before taking something else out. Similarly, reps only have a certain amount of time to sell your products/services; they usually represent a full complement of lines. You are competing for your reps' time.

So how do you get your reps to focus on presenting you? PRO members have developed several strategies. One strategy is to have an employee regularly work with reps in the field. The rep provides the sales expertise; the employee provides the product expertise. More important, during the time they are together, the rep is virtually forced to present your products/services, setting appointments with existing accounts and targeted prospects.

Don't have someone to send into the field? You need to motivate your reps! Here are some of the things PRO members do:

- Reps are most likely to present the products/services that are easiest to sell. Make sure they're yours! Develop marketing programs that support your reps' efforts. This might include providing cooperative advertising dollars, discounts, ready-made displays, and/or catalog allowances—all of which boost sales and give reps something to talk about with accounts.
- Reps are most likely to present the products/services that generate the greatest rewards. Develop rewards that will capture their enthusiasm. Each rep organization you work with might have a different trigger; it's your job to determine what that is. Is it a bonus commission? A trip to some exotic locale? The pride

of professional excellence—i.e., recognition? If you are not one of your reps' major sources of income, it is difficult to make demands on them.

- Sell reps on your company. Take the time to teach them about your programs, products, and services. Emphasize the support you provide to them and the quality you offer customers. If they are not sold on you, your company's products will remain only a page in their notebooks. Some reps will have a natural affinity for your products or services. These are gems. Treat them especially well.
- Iron out known problems in your sales process. Reps don't want to have problems and won't present a company they perceive to be problematic.

It's not enough to add or replace manufacturers reps. To get the most out of them, motivate them just as much as you motivate your employees.

In summary, your salespeople are your company's foot soldiers. If they fall, the company cannot succeed. Start to finish, it's your job to ensure their victory. It's up to you to map out a winning sales strategy, then choose the right recruits and prepare them for battle.

CHAPTER FOUR

MARKETING

In many small companies, "sales" and "marketing" are lumped together, when in fact they are two distinct activities and disciplines. Salespeople are on the front lines, directly engaged with customers. The marketing staff stands behind them, providing the intelligence, tools, and programs that drive and support their efforts.

In other words, if salespeople are your foot soldiers, marketing represents the Ordinance Department. It is marketing's responsibility to arm the troops with the ammo they need through branding, differentiation, and a multitude of tactics. It is marketing's job to stake out a winning position on the field.

BRANDING, POSITIONING, AND DIFFERENTIATION

There is no value in being a "me too!" company. To grow, you must set your company apart. You do this by taking a unique position, differentiating yourself from your competition, and reinforcing your identity through consistent branding.

Even if you sell a commodity product (like concrete), you can differentiate your company by servicing your customers in a unique way. In order to build your company, you must also build your brand.

Achieving Differentiation—What Are You Willing to Give Up?

Differentiation is essential to small business success. It is common, however, to confuse branding and differentiation. What's the difference?

When you create a branding statement, you are carving out an identity for your company. You are painting a picture of how you'd like your company to be perceived. But no small business can be all things to all people. Differentiation is what sets you apart from your competition. When you differentiate, you take a specific position. It absolutely cannot be the same position as your competitor. (If you take the same position as your competitor, you only reinforce your competitor's strength.)

In order to make an impact, you must position yourself within narrow perimeters. If it is too wide or too encompassing, all you will achieve is confusion. Yes, it's difficult to give up a market, but remember: your business is a small business. You have limited resources and finances. In order to make an impact, you must go niche, limit, and give up some market sectors.

I offer you my own company, PRO, as an example. PRO, or President's Resource Organization, creates peer advisory boards just for small business leaders. When establishing PRO, I could have taken the position that PRO creates peer advisory boards for business leaders, period.

But I chose to give up the medium and large business sectors so I could focus on the small business owner. I then created a program that specifically addresses the needs of the small business owner. Giving up the medium and large business sectors freed me to become a small business specialist. That gives me a more compelling story to tell and also provides a clear target for my marketing efforts.

In the car rental world, Hertz is known as the largest agency. Avis, on the other hand, has taken the position that "We Try Harder." Avis has further reinforced its differentiation by becoming an employee-owned company. The premise: when you deal with an Avis employee, you're actually dealing with an owner. As an owner, that person would naturally "try harder." It's a brilliant differentiation strategy.

You can do the same for your company. If your competition has already taken a position, find another one for yourself. If your competition has not taken a clear position, you have the freedom to differentiate yourself however you like. Choose the position you want, and be ready to leave the others behind.

Pricing and Positioning Strategies

Pricing and positioning go hand in hand. Pricing should be driven by your marketing position and differentiation strategy.

Do you want to be known as the company that's easiest to deal with? The one with the unconditional guarantee? The one that provides the best management information (if yours is a service company)? The one that provides "live" status updates? All these things—plus your products or services, commitment to quality, and the way you service your customers—help establish your market position, which in turn should drive your pricing.

In general, for small businesses, pricing should be predicated on what the market will bear, not cost multiples. Some companies price from a formula. The problem with formula pricing is that costing is a highly complicated process. Many companies fail to take all factors into account. For example, how do you apply overhead? How do you price the administrative cost of implementing and managing multiple small projects, as opposed to one larger project? Ask a hundred cost accountants to price a given manufacturer's product and you may end up with a hundred different costs—all of which could be ably defended as the "true cost."

Rather than target a gross profit percentage or minimum gross profit dollar contribution per job, most PRO members recommend pricing to what the market will bear. If you have a formula price, mark it as the lowest price you will ever offer. Know your product or service, your customer, and your company. Base your pricing on what the market wants and what it will tolerate.

Warning! Never Aim to Be the Lowest-Cost Company

However you want to position your company, avoid positioning yourself as the company with the lowest prices. Many new PRO members confess to this goal, and it's one the rest of us quickly talk them out of!

Why? Well, for one thing, it's highly unlikely that your small business will ever be in a position to produce products more cost-effectively than the big boys. It's simple economies of scale. And for another, why in the world would you want to be known as The Cheapest Company Around? Wouldn't you rather be known as The Company That Delivers the Best Value? Value, of course, is the sum of all the attributes of the sales transaction: price, quality, delivery, ease of working with you, understanding of the customer's need, service, upgrades, field maintenance, hassle factors, etc. Doesn't that make more sense?

Sometimes low pricing can be used to buy into targeted markets. If you use this strategy, be careful to use it judiciously. It is a dangerous habit to get into. Use it only in select situations and with a defined percentage of revenues.

Remember, PRO members consider pricing part of their strategy for achieving goals—whether those goals are a utilization of production capacity, protecting market position, or maximizing profitability.

Here's an interesting example. PRO member Stuart, who owns a plastics manufacturing company, was in the enviable situation where demand exceeded capacity. The normal response would be to purchase more capacity—in his case, very expensive machinery. Instead, he elected to raise his prices, therefore reducing demand and maximizing the profitability of his machine center.

Linda's company, on the other hand, is technology driven. Her pricing strategy is to lower her prices as her product is accepted in the marketplace. Her objective? By removing the price umbrella, she discourages competition to enter the field. Products with low barriers of entry are forced to work with low margins.

If you want to achieve higher margins, work on differentiating your company and products. One of our PRO members owns two companies that operate independently. Both companies provide the same product. However, one company is perceived by the market to offer a very high level of quality—and therefore achieves a substantially higher margin. The other company, which offers equal quality but is not perceived as top-drawer, offers competitive pricing.

The point is, *you* can control your pricing, and price setting should be determined by your company's goals.

Defining Your Customer

We've urged you to define your brand identity and your position of differentiation. Now it's time to define your customer.

Because you have a small business, "everyone" can't be your customer. You have limited resources. Your customers should be limited, too.

Defining your customer affects every aspect of your business. If you are a retailer, for example, your customer will determine the location of your outlet, the type of merchandise you carry, the type of promotions you feature, and even the sales help you hire.

You can define your customer a number of ways. If your customers are consumers, you can use demographic information, such as age, gender, income, job type, or geographic location. You can also define them in terms of ethnicity, health issues, interests, or buying patterns—whatever factor makes them of interest to you. B-to-B customers can also be characterized in a variety of ways, such as industry, business size, SIC code, financial strength, or by the products and services they sell.

One PRO member has a company that produces injection-molded promotional products. This company's skill is the ability to create unique, inexpensive items that customers give away as retail promotions. The PRO member has defined his customer as a mass producer of retail products—one that is marketing oriented, has a large promotional budget, and is looking for unique solutions that create end-customer demand. This customer does not sell industrial molded products, high-tolerance engineered plastics, or short-run items. Because the PRO member has defined his customer so precisely, he can concentrate his marketing efforts on the three hundred to five hundred companies that meet his definition.

In some cases, it makes sense to create a psychological profile of your target customer. For example, the ideal PRO "customer" is a small business owner, CEO, COO, or partner, with company revenues between $500,000 and $20,000,000. But that's not all. In addition, in order to appreciate the benefits of PRO, the prospect must be open to new ideas, have a desire to learn, be willing to share his or her knowledge, and be willing to accept criticism. In this case, the customer is defined by psychological criteria as much as title and business size.

Not sure who your target customer is? Start by analyzing your current customer base. What are the common traits of your best customers? That's the basis of your definition. Once you've defined your customer, you can determine how to appeal to others like him or her.

Mind Share, Market Share
Mind share leads to market share.

Mind share is what your prospects and customers think about you. If you're like virtually all PRO members, you want to boost mind share—i.e., increase awareness of your company and its offerings.

How do you grow mind share? By employing a wide range of complementary marketing and sales activities, from advertising to trade show participation to actively seeking publicity.

Gaining mind share is critical. But remember, it is not your ultimate objective. Mind share is really just a means to the end, which is, of course, increasing market share. Furthermore, mind share will not result in increased market share unless your efforts are directly targeted to your defined customer.

How can you determine if your marketing awareness programs are successful—to see if mind share is growing? The most scientific way is to measure it over the course of time. You begin by taking a baseline measurement—that is, measuring public awareness of your company and your products as it stands today. Do your customers perceive your company the way you want them to? With a baseline measurement, you learn how your defined customer defines *you*. Once you have that baseline, you can evaluate the effectiveness of all future marketing initiatives against it by measuring public awareness on an ongoing basis.

You can measure more than the effectiveness of your own marketing initiatives. You can see how your company stacks up against the competition in your customers' minds, focusing on those characteristics you believe to be most crucial to the buying decision.

Unfortunately, market research is not something you can do on your own. A flawed process—from asking the wrong questions to incorrectly evaluating the answers—will yield skewed results or meaningless information.

To do it right, you need to call on a skilled market research firm, both to create the baseline measurement and to conduct subsequent studies. This is not an inexpensive proposition for a small business. But if your company is marketing driven, it may be worthwhile to you. It's certainly worth your consideration.

Of course, the ultimate test of mind share is market share—the true measure of your company's total success. According to Harvard University's landmark PIMS study, *market share is the number one criteria of profitability.*

General Electric Corporation—always worth studying—has adopted a fascinating approach to the managing of its many divisions. If a division is not first or second in its given market, that division goes on the auction block. According to GE, market share is so important—and so expensive and difficult to increase—that divisions that don't make the cut aren't profitable enough to keep.

In attempting to determine your market share, you must first define the market you want to measure, both in terms of product/service range and market demographics.

How do you measure market share? If you belong to a trade association, the association may already be doing the work for you. Many associations calculate the total market of its products and services.

But what if all indications point to a cold truth: that you do not hold a major position of market share? How do you change things? According to the PIMS study, a company's best strategy is to promote quality as a means of gaining mind share and, ultimately, market share.

Branding a Service

Your "brand" is how your company is perceived. Your brand is generated not only through marketing activities, but more important, through every point of contact your customers experience. The objective of branding is to attract customers by creating value in their minds for whatever it is you are providing.

Branding a service company is trickier than branding a company that manufacturers or sells tangible products. Why? Because your customers don't have concrete attributes to measure and compare. As a result, the value they place on your service is more subjective in nature.

Now that has not prevented PRO members in service industries from branding their companies and offerings. Their secret? Differentiate your company from your competition by naming and defining the process you employ. It could be the same process used by everyone in your industry, but by promoting it, you transform it into a unique and special advantage that customers can get only from you. The customers are made to feel that they are somehow receiving better, smarter, or faster results.

But before you start defining and promoting your process, be sure you "live the process" as well. What does that mean? Every touch with the customer—from the first inquiry to the invoice they receive for services rendered—must be consistent with your process. In other words, every point of contact must underscore your brand. If not, your branding message will sound a false note with your customers. So it is important to get your ducks in a row from the outset. If you're successful at this, you help move the buying decision from a subjective one to an objective one. The value is there in your living, breathing branding statement.

There's another advantage to branding your service: it's a boon to any exit strategy. Should you decide to sell your business, a branding position offers greater value. Your business is not just another service company! Usually personnel are considered the service company's greatest asset. Successful branding will help you attract more qualified employees, who also buy into the brand. When it comes time to exit, you will have two notable assets to offer: outstanding employees and a recognized branding position.

CASE STUDY: AARON

Aaron is a builder who specializes in custom residential homes. There are a number of small custom builders in his area and competition is fierce. Aaron wanted a way to make his company stand out.

Aaron recognized that his industry isn't typically process-oriented. He also identified that one of his chief challenges is communicating with customers. Many customers delay making decisions on a timely basis, holding up the entire project. So Aaron developed a formal communication program that leads customers through each stage of the building process on a fixed schedule. He named it, branded it, and designed marketing materials promoting his program.

Now when Aaron is bidding against another builder, he has a powerful advantage. He has something extra to offer and appears more professional than his competition. Aaron not only branded his business, he solved one of his biggest challenges!

THE MARKETING PLAN

A surprising number of small businesses go to market in a haphazard way. They don't have an organized marketing plan or budget. Working from inspiration and impulse, they get sidetracked by tactics, which are activities not linked to specific objectives (more on tactics in the following pages). There is no big picture, no defined long-term objective other than "to succeed." The problem is, how can a slipshod approach to marketing result in anything other than slapdash results?

Creating a Marketing Plan and Budget

Marketing is so important to business success that it's certainly worth devoting your time and resources to crafting a plan. A marketing plan is not a sales activity plan, but rather everything outside the actual sales process. Marketing is used to generate leads, establish branding, grow mind share, and create differentiation—in other words, all those activities that complement and support your sales process.

We've already discussed the necessity of defining your customer, positioning, and branding. When it comes to developing a marketing plan, the first step is to define your objectives. Ask yourself the following questions:

- What do I want to achieve? (And why do I want to achieve it?)
- Who do I want to sell to?
- What products or services do I specifically want to sell?
- What price do I want to sell them at?
- By what percentage do I want to increase sales?

When it comes to marketing programs, you have infinite options, from direct mail to trade shows to advertising to publicity. (You can examine these more closely in "Creating a Full-Blown Communications Program," on page 119.) You must decide which of these options will be both effective and cost effective. And you can't weigh your options until they are written down. Then choices and alternatives become clear. (Expect the first draft of your marketing plan to vary widely from the final version.)

In addition to itemizing the specific initiatives you will take, your marketing plan should contain the following components:

- *Budget*—A shocking number of new PRO members admit they have no formal marketing budget; they just spend money when they think it's a good idea. If you don't have a firm budget, you don't have a real plan. You will end up spending too little or too much on hit-and-miss marketing efforts. Furthermore, break your budget down into components—

say, production versus the cost of the actual marketing activity. For example, if you decide to undertake an advertising campaign, you will be paying both production costs (the cost to get those ads written and designed) and placement costs (the cost charged by magazines, newspapers, etc., to run the ads).

- *Expected Results*—Express these in terms of dollars sold, number of new leads, expanded mind share, or whatever way makes sense in relation to your goal. If you don't state your goal in measurable terms, how can you determine the value and effectiveness of your marketing activities?

- *Schedule*—Attaching deadlines to each initiative in your plan ensures it will actually get done. It also ensures a year of steady, consistent marketing activity—not a crazed reaction to a dip in sales or a flurry of year-end panic.

- *Accountability*—Delegating segments of the plan to specific employees will make the plan more achievable, while creating an opportunity to measure performance. You can also benefit from the synergy of shared ideas and the camaraderie of a group effort.

Your marketing plan is like a product blueprint or an architect's drawing. It's an organized process that minimizes risk while helping you get the biggest bang for your buck. It ensures that all your marketing efforts send a consistent, branded message. It also eliminates impulse decision making. And, most important, it pushes you closer to your goals.

TACTICS

When you create a marketing plan, you determine your priorities and define your objectives. Once those are established, you can employ specific tactics that will best help you achieve your goals. Tactics are not an end in themselves, but they are invaluable marketing tools. Here are some ideas for your toolbox.

Trade Shows: Before, During, and After

Often at PRO meetings, a member will announce that he or she is sponsoring a booth at an upcoming trade show. Inevitably, the facilitator will respond with this question: "What do you want to accomplish there?"

Companies exhibit at trade shows for all kinds of reasons: to touch base with old customers, attract new ones, introduce new products or services, or maintain/raise visibility within the industry. However, "Because we do it every year!" is not a valid reason.

Trade show exhibitions represent a large investment for a small business. Consider the total costs: booth expenses, freight to ship the booth and merchandise, travel and entertainments costs—not to mention your loss of time and activity! After all, if you and your staff are at the trade show, you're not getting work done at home.

Trade shows can be very beneficial, but they are not something you should attend out of habit. You should always have a defined goal you wish to achieve by attending, a goal that justifies the expense.

Suppose you determine that you do have a goal and that it is worth investing in. Then it is also worth developing a strategy for accomplishing it. Let's face it—it's always easier to jump headfirst into implementation than it is to plan a careful strategy. Yet planning such a strategy will maximize your results, boosting your trade show ROI.

Your strategy for sales/marketing activities can be divided into three segments: those to be conducted before, during, and after the show. Obviously, creating the strategy is in itself the largest chunk of your pre-show activities. Here are some ideas to consider:

Pre-Show Activities

- Promote your attendance at the show. Alert customers and prospects that you will be attending, either through postcards, emails, or your customer newsletter. Encourage them to visit your booth, perhaps by offering a contest or promotion.
- A national trade show is an ideal time to touch base with clients and contacts you don't see very often. Set up appointments in advance, to be held either at your booth, at a restaurant, or at some other location in the host city.
- Make sure your booth is ready—that it's attractive, eye-catching, and up-to-date.
- Don't wait until the last minute to select the marketing materials and samples you'll bring along. These, too, should reflect well on you and your products. Never got around to creating the one marketing piece

you really need to promote your products effectively? Trade shows are a great incentive to get things done, but you need enough lead time to get them produced.

- Devise a strategy for collecting contact information on future prospects. Holding a prize drawing (and offering a prize of some value) is one way to get prospects to part with their business cards.

- Trade shows offer once-a-year advertising opportunities, either in the show book or in industry trade pubs that will be widely distributed at the show. Would it make sense to advertise in them? If so, plan your ad message carefully and have the ad ready by the publication close dates.

- You know what your goal is—plan additional activities that will help you achieve it.

During the Show Activities

If you've done a good job of advance planning, you're in good shape to make the most of every hour of the show. This includes turning meals into client meetings, successfully engaging visitors at your booth, and connecting with as many contacts as possible. Keep your goal in mind throughout the show, so you can work toward accomplishing it.

If your goal is to enhance client relationships, sponsor events that enable you to spend time with them. Golf outings are popular, provided your clients are golfers. Obviously, you'll want to choose activities of interest to key clients. For example, one PRO member sponsors poker parties because it goes over well with his most important clients.

Jot down notes as you meet with various clients and prospects. It's a good idea to review your notes at the end of each day, expanding and clarifying on your scribbles. This way, when you get back home you'll know exactly what follow-up action is required.

In addition, don't overlook the opportunity to catch up on the industry buzz. Check out your competition and see what they're up to. Bring comfortable shoes and take your vitamins: it's showtime!

Post-Show Activities

These, too, should be planned in advance. Before you even leave for the show, anticipate what you will do upon your immediate return. For example, make sure you have follow-up materials on hand and sample product ready to ship. Put your staff on high alert. There is only a short window of response time after the trade show before the momentum starts to fade. Seize the moment!

- Follow up with customers and prospects, providing details and answers to questions that were raised during your meetings. Do this quickly upon your return, while the subject is still fresh in everyone's minds.
- If you collected business cards during the show (and you would be foolish not to), follow up swiftly with these prospects, too, either with a letter or phone call.
- Play Monday morning quarterback—review your performance at the trade show. Was your booth a

> success, or are improvements required? Were your handouts effective? Did your advertising make an impact? How did your meetings go—should you have scheduled more of them? Most important, do you think you achieved your goal?

Trade shows can be tremendously helpful if you attend them for the right reasons and prepare for them carefully. Treat your next trade show like a Broadway opening, and you can garner rave reviews.

Using Public Relations: Let the World Know!

Some PRO members are natural-born publicity hounds; others are terrified of seeking the limelight. The fact is that public relations (or PR) can be a highly effective form of marketing. Think about it. When a newspaper casts the spotlight on a local business, it looks like an endorsement, and that's invaluable. Unlike paid advertising, PR gives you that coveted third-party credibility. Getting your company's name in the media is a surefire way to reach a larger segment of potential customers.

But here's something you need to know about public relations: the media are interested in particular kinds of stories. It is not enough to say, "Here's my business— look at me!" You can't assume that just because you find your company fascinating, the media will too. That's why it's often helpful to enlist the aid of a publicist—particularly one who specializes in promoting small businesses. A publicist knows what kind of stories to pitch and which editors to pitch them to. Consultations are usually free; consider lining up one or two, if only to get a better understanding of how PR works.

Think the cost of a publicist is out of your reach? It doesn't have to be. While most big PR firms insist on retainers, many independent publicists charge hourly or by-the-project rates. For small businesses, these are generally a much better deal. As with any outside consultant, be sure the scope of the project is fully defined from the beginning.

The bottom line is: newspapers cover news. To get some, you have to make some. If you have an unusual business or product, it's easier to attract publicity. If you don't, find an interesting angle. For example, if you have a CPA firm, offer your local newspaper editors some tax tips (do this just before tax season arrives). If you own a restaurant, send the food editor some of your favorite recipes, along with a brief history of your personal culinary experience.

Here are some other ideas to get you thinking:

- Review your local newspapers. Note the various sections. Who writes the articles? If you can see yourself featured in a particular section, send your article idea or "press release" to that journalist.
- Trend stories are a wonderful way to get plugged into an article. (This means you aren't the focus of the article, but a part of it.) If something interesting is happening in your industry, alert the business editor. Perhaps you can put a local spin on a national trend—and land an interview in the process.

- Don't neglect business journals in your area—their mission is to cover your community's business news. Have you recently opened a new location? Begun offering a new product or service? These are newsworthy. Even corporate anniversaries and "people and promotions" bits can get your company's name in the papers.
- Want to enhance your industry recognition? Write up an article for your favorite trade publications. Be ready to provide a current business photo and a two-sentence biography. You'll usually get a byline—and the admiration of your peers. (Bonus: you can use reprints of your article as marketing tools.)
- The media loves good-works stories. If you are volunteering your products or services to a local charity, share the news not only with newspapers, but local television news channels. TV is filled with heart-warming visual segments…why not be one of them?
- When talking to the media, learn how to speak in *sound bites*—short, snappy sentences that are highly quotable. Avoid rambling. Stay on point. If you give the reporter the quote she is looking for, she'll call on you the next time she needs an expert in your field.

One last thing to remember about publicity: unlike paid advertising, you can't control the final product. You may give a one-hour interview, only to receive a one-sentence quote in the finished article. You may find the reporter ignores your brilliant key points and focuses on something you barely remember saying. There is some uncertainty that comes with the territory.

But for those who learn to work it, PR can be an invaluable marketing tool.

Making Your Ideas Contagious

Upon first joining PRO, many new members immediately announce that they "don't do marketing." They proudly tell us that their business is generated solely by referrals and word-of-mouth.

Word-of-mouth advertising is a very good thing. In fact, it's such a good thing that you shouldn't leave it to chance. Why sit back and wait for any old prospect to find you when you can proactively create a buzz that has the right prospects flocking to your door?

Experienced PRO members take word-of-mouth advertising to the next level by consciously making their ideas, products, and services "contagious." They recommend spreading the news about your company like a virus—a healthy, beneficial virus, of course.

Speaking of viruses, the Internet is an ideal way to spread your news because of its very low cost per point of contact. Distributing an ongoing e-newsletter—one that provides information of value—is a great way to boost word of mouth. Take care, however, that your e-newsletter will not be perceived as spam. (How? By choosing your audience carefully, offering genuine content, and utilizing opt-in lists, for starters.)

For example, my organization, PRO, distributes a free monthly e-newsletter that introduces a "PRO-vocative Idea of the Month." A microcosm of an actual PRO meeting, the newsletter presents a common business problem followed by discussion (in the form of comments provided by actual members) and solutions. The professionally designed newsletter always concludes with one suggestion. Readers forward it to their colleagues and associates. There's a double benefit here: PRO members can use the newsletter as a vehicle for connecting with others, while the PRO message gets more widely dispersed.

In essence, this is a form of *sampling*—giving away a product or service in order to get people talking about it. Many large companies use sampling to create a buzz with the consumer, from enclosing a packet of hand cream in your Sunday paper to offering taste tests at your local supermarket. If you sell a service instead of a product, you can offer samples of your expertise and knowledge in the form of shared information.

To create a bona fide "virus," however, your product or service must be different, meaningful, or interesting. (Advertising specialty items—such as pens, mugs, and Post-Its—will supposedly keep your name in front of the customer. But after years and years of overuse, these trinkets are hardly breakthrough.) A prime example of such contagious ideas is, appropriately enough, the book *Unleashing the Ideavirus* by Seth Godin—the most frequently downloaded book in Internet history. Originally available as a free download, it ultimately became a bestseller because of proactive word of mouth. Now also available in book form, it is filled with infectious virus ideas that you can "catch" and use.

Creating a Full-Blown Communications Program

Once you have developed your product or service, the logical next step is to create a brochure extolling its virtues. The problem is that once that brochure is written, many entrepreneurs think their marketing communications work is done. The truth is, that sales brochure should be just the first step in a multifaceted, ongoing program.

There are many ways to tell your story and various audiences to tell it to. Your sales brochure should be supported by multiple marketing initiatives, including:

- Advertising (print, radio, and Internet banner ads).
- Collateral materials (identity brochures, sales sheets, and direct mail pieces, such as postcards, self-mailers, and flyers).
- Internet marketing (a spiffy website, email newsletters, search engine marketing, and affiliate partnership programs).
- Ongoing customer communications (newsletters, fax bulletins, even simple letters and service phone calls).
- Publicity (get your product, service, and face featured in local newspapers, national magazines, and on radio and TV. Boost industry awareness by writing articles for trade publications).
- Trade show advertising (have a booth, offer samples, put on a demonstration, and generally create a consistent industry presence).

It is also essential to recognize and appeal directly to your various audiences. It's often wise to craft separate communications for customers, sales reps, employees, prospects—even your vendors. Each may need to hear your story from a different perspective. How does it benefit them specifically?

When it comes to communications, employees tend to get overlooked. Create a company newsletter or bulletin. Feature success stories, an "employee of the month," or other morale-building content. Make sure everyone's always up-to-date on your products and processes. For example, if you're running an ad campaign, make sure your staff is the first to know. An employee should never learn company news from a customer or vendor.

One way to stay on top of your communications program is to create a communications calendar. One PRO member constructs a comprehensive annual calendar, using different colored inks to represent each audience—customer, employee, etc. This ensures that communication takes place regularly on every level and that new goals are continually established and met. Communication is not a single sales brochure. Just like sales, it's an ongoing endeavor.

Mining for Treasure: Database Mining

Studies show that it is easier and less expensive to get additional business from existing customers than to continually market to new prospects. That's why it's important to know about your customers, their needs, and their buying habits. The more you know, the better you can position your company to meet more of those needs. That knowledge is an invaluable treasure.

Do you have a method to catalog, store, and access such priceless information?

Think about your local grocery store. Almost every large chain employs an in-house discount card. Yes, that card provides you, the customer, with ongoing discounts and check-cashing privileges. But it provides the chain with something even more valuable: the ability to track how much you purchase, how often you purchase, and what you purchase. Big Brother is "mining" you! And that allows Big Brother to create marketing programs that make you a more frequent and loyal shopper.

It is unrealistic to expect a small business to go to this extreme. But knowing more about your customers' buying habits can help you maximize service, value, and loyalty. Knowing how frequently—and at what quantity—major customers purchase particular items can be instrumental in managing scheduling, inventory, and servicing activities well.

Many PRO members use CSM (customer service management) software to help them gather information. They report excellent results. Such software allows you to measure business received against potential business that can be achieved by serving more of your clients' needs. And isn't that what it's all about? In addition, such detailed customer information will ultimately become an asset, in the form of intellectual property. Should you decide to sell your business, this information can help you place a value on it.

If you want something simpler, consider a software program like Goldmine or ACT. These allow you to capture basic information about your customers and their buying patterns. They give you the option of creating variable fields so you can easily record information of interest to you.

In addition, train your sales and service people to document conversations with customers. Along with their buying history, customers' comments and complaints can give you tremendous insight into their wants and needs.

Put on your miner's helmet and turn on the light. Determine what information you need to know about your customers and their buying habits. Set up a procedure for capturing this information. Analyze the results. Then build sales and marketing plans to mine that untapped business. Thar's gold in them thar databases!

The Gift That Keeps on Giving: Donating Your Products or Services to Charity

PRO member Sharon owns a print shop. Each year, Sharon selects a charity she believes in. She approaches the charity and offers it a fixed dollar amount of free printing. Without fail, the charity takes Sharon up on her offer. Without fail, she receives additional business from that charity over and above the amount of her donation.

In essence, Sharon has created a sampling program. The potential customers—in this case, the charities—get the opportunity to experience the quality and service Sharon's print shop provides, motivating them to return as a paying customer. Over the years, Sharon has expanded her client base by using this strategy.

Think about it: charities and not-for-profits are always seeking ways to raise revenues. Developing programs that benefit them can also benefit you. It also allows you to contribute to your favorite causes and may offer some tax benefits.

So you don't own a print shop. What can you offer them? Well, many not-for-profits hold auctions to raise funds. You can provide them with merchandise or services to be auctioned. This gives you exposure, both to not-for-profits and their supporters. Such sampling may lead to additional business. And of course you're creating goodwill.

Here's another way to go about it. Perhaps you have a target prospect that is deeply connected to a particular not-for-profit. Approach the prospect with your offer of free goods or services for his or her pet charity. It might just be the door opener you need to land the account.

It makes sense to make cents for not-for-profits...provided you carefully pick and choose those that offer a good return on your investment.

An organized marketing program is the key to establishing a competitive position. Nevertheless, many small businesses fail to appreciate its importance. Failure to brand and differentiate a company put it at risk for eventual failure. Similarly, engaging in haphazard tactics is a waste of time and money. Your marketing efforts should be targeted, coordinated, and, most of all, planned. If failure is not an option, marketing shouldn't be either.

CHAPTER FIVE

PERFORMANCE AND ORGANIZATION

In today's highly competitive world, implementation and performance are everything. As a result, your employees are either your company's most powerful asset or its greatest liability.

How do you ensure that your employees are the former, not the latter? By focusing on their performance, individually and as a whole. In other words, by creating performance standards, conducting evaluations, rewarding people who measure up, and releasing those who do not. It also means continually evaluating your organizational structure to ensure it supports your goals. For most small business owners, these activities don't come easily, yet they are critical to ongoing success. If you're not already doing them, it's time to get started.

ORGANIZATION CONCEPTS AND STRUCTURE

When it comes to organizational structure, there is no single right answer. If your company's structure supports your current and long-term objectives, then it's right for you. However, in many small companies structure takes on a life of its own. It's up to you, the business owner, to consciously define and shape your organization. It's up to you to put the right people in place and perfect your processes. That means measuring, planning, and looking ahead to the future.

Creating Measurable Standards

If you can't measure it, you can't manage it, either. How do employees know if they're doing a good job? How can you know what your company's capabilities are?

Too many small companies manage by the seat of their pants, using guesswork, wishful thoughts, and intuition. In order to manage a business properly, you need to create processes and performance measurements.

Most companies find it easiest to measure sales because it's so black-and-white—either you get the business or you don't. The sales funnel, discussed earlier, helps measure each step of the sales process.

But it's important to look beyond sales, creating measurable standards and objectives for every aspect of your business. Once they exist, these standards can not only help measure performance, but identify trends and potential problems before they get out of hand.

Here's a checklist of some of the specific measurements PRO members use to evaluate their companies:

CASH FLOW	Accounts receivable: # of days outstanding Accounts receivable: % 30 days, 60 days, and 90 days uncollected Accounts receivable: average collection time period Inventory turnover ratio: # of days inventory is on hand
CUSTOMER SERVICE	Daily expected orders, compared to actual backorder % .# of days it takes to fill an order % of on-time delivery or project completion
PRODUCTION	Actual production compared to standard Actual set-up time compared to standard % of reworks or rejects, measured in pieces or $$$ FTEs (full-time equivalents) compared to peer information (check with your trade association for availability of information)
FINANCIAL	Gross profit compared to budget/standard Actual overhead % or $$$ compared to budget/standard % of major expense categories compared to budget/standard for sales, general, and administrative expenses Net profit % or $$$ compared to budget/standard

MARKETING	# of leads generated/cost per lead
	Timeliness of project completion
	Actual $$$ spent compared to budget
ACCOUNTING	# of adjustments made by outside auditors
	# of days to complete financial statement after close of month/quarter/year
PURCHASING	Positive purchase variances compared to budget/standard

This is just a partial list, but you get the idea. And although many people complain that it's difficult to measure staff activities such as marketing, accounting, and purchasing, you see it is possible.

Add these rulers to your toolbox and you can manage your business while avoiding potential problems. Is there a cost? Yes. Measuring these activities can increase some administrative costs. Is it a worthwhile investment? Yes. At the very least, create measurements for your company's problem areas—as well as everywhere where the potential savings outweigh costs.

Crafting a Three-Year Organization Chart

One of our PRO members came up with an intriguing—and eye-opening—tool for moving his company forward: the three-year organization chart. That's right: an organization chart that projects three years into the future.

Most small business owners don't even have a current organization chart, let alone a future one. Or if they do, it's built around the people and personalities they happen to have in place. This type of organization chart will tell you where you are, but it won't take you where you want to be. (Don't have one? Map one out—you're going to need it to complete this exercise.)

Now, here's the beauty of the three-year organization chart: in order to create it, you have to first define your long-term business goals. Where do you want the company to be three years down the road? Your three-year organization chart reflects what the company will have to look like in order to support the goals you've established. (Remember, the three-year organization chart should not be structured around your current personnel, but what the company will actually need in order to fulfill your three-year goals.)

Obviously, the three-year organization chart is not set in stone. It's only a guide. In creating it, you have to make a number of assumptions. Document these assumptions so you can test their validity going forward. You will see if the chart still stands.

It's important to structure your three-year organization chart around your number one goal. Know that your structure will vary according to your number one priority. Is it technology? Market environment? Processes? Each will call for a different organizational structure.

Now comes the moment of truth: compare your three-year organization chart to your current one. Beware...this can be a real shocker! You may discover, to your horror, that you have the wrong people in the wrong places.

Don't let this possibility skew your charting. Ultimately, this knowledge is the very thing you need to get on the right track. Look at it this way: the more unpleasant the truth is, the more you need to know it. Only then can you start taking steps to correct your direction. Now you know where you're going *and* which road will take you there.

Raising the Bar

Are you truly satisfied with the way your employees are performing? Or do you routinely accept average and below-average performance? It's easy to become complacent; it's hard to make changes. If you're like many small employers, you'd like to raise the bar but you don't know how.

PRO members have found that the way to raise the bar is to change expectations. What's the first step? It may seem obvious, but the first thing to do is to define what a "good job" is for your employees. Too often, small companies have vague expectations. How can employees perform a good job—let alone a great job—when it's never been defined for them?

Frankly, it is rare for a small business to create measurements for success. It's even rarer for one to make changes when success is not achieved. It is not easy or comfortable, but it is worthwhile.

Once you've created measurements, you have a tool for evaluating acceptable performance. Now employees can be held accountable. However, you must be held accountable too, by providing the training and communication your employees need to perform to a higher standard.

And you must be willing to make changes (e.g., transfer tasks or let people go) when employees don't perform.

General Electric Corporation has what might seem like an extreme HR policy. Each year, it replaces the bottom 10 percent of the management team. Seems harsh, doesn't it? Yes, but it automatically raises performance expectations on an annual basis. A manager who is evaluated in the upper 50 percent can find himself dropping to the cut-off point in just a few years. Needless to say, this keeps everyone on his or her toes.

I'm not suggesting this will work as a model for you. Most small business owners strive to create a "family" feeling within the ranks. That's fine—but not when it means keeping underachievers on the payroll.

Another way to raise the bar is to get your employees more invested in the business. This means openly sharing your visions and goals and obtaining employee buy-in on initiatives and solutions. Do it and eventually they'll be creating solutions for you!

Creating an open dialogue fosters success, raising the bar not just for employees, but also for the company.

Starring and Supporting Roles

A winning company is like a winning basketball team. The team has a few shining stars, backed by a bench of solid, supporting players. The stars make those stunning half-court shots. The supporting players allow them to by providing strong defense, playing their positions, and handing off the ball at the right moment.

Realistically, it's impossible to have nothing but all-stars. For one thing, stars are very hard to find. For another, they can be hard to work with, and even harder to manage. A well-run team is made up of stars and supporting players working together. Your company is such a team.

Look at your company from this point of view. What are your starring roles? Where must your organization excel—in sales, marketing, or product development? Think of your goals and your driving force.

This knowledge can impact your hiring decisions. Too often, we settle for the "best" candidate instead of the right candidate. We accept average talent because that's what presents itself. In key positions, this simply isn't good enough. When it comes to starring roles, you need someone who can shoot the ball.

In virtually all small companies, the business owner is the brightest star, at least initially. As PRO member Stan says, "My job is to make waves. My staff's job is to smooth them out." Yin and yang. Peanut butter and jelly. It takes both stars and supporting teammates to pull off a win.

Don't Hire Anyone You Can't Fire

You want to hire your best friend. You think he would be good for the company. Is this a wise thing to do? Probably not. If your best friend doesn't work out or meet expectations, you will have a bad employee *and* a ruined relationship.

This includes relatives, friends, neighbors, and their offspring. Yes, it's nice to do a friend a favor when someone needs a job, but you do so at the expense of your company and your friendship. You are wedging yourself firmly between a rock and a hard place.

If they don't perform, what are your options?

You will be forced to choose between your relationship with this person and your duty to your organization. Either way, you lose. Either you keep the employee and dilute your company, or you let him or her go and create hard feelings. One or the other of you will become bitter and disenchanted. (Sometimes this happens in partnerships over time. As the parties grow, they develop different goals or crave different life experiences. This is especially true when the enterprise is successful.)

Recently, a PRO member confessed that he wanted to hire his brother-in-law. His fellow members urged him to examine the situation fully, to define his expectations, and to consider his future goals. *Think, think, and think again,* they said. Try to avoid this temptation at all costs. How can you really be sure that person will perform?

Ah, but what if you've already hired someone you know and it isn't working out? There is a brilliant way to get rid of them without creating a rift. To learn the secret, read "The Politically Correct Way to Get Rid of a Political Problem," in chapter 6 (see page 180).

CASE STUDY: SAM

Over the objections of his fellow PRO members, Sam hired his younger brother. He's always looked out for his brother, and his brother needed a job.

Sam's brother wasn't really qualified for the position. Not surprisingly, he didn't produce. Reluctantly, Sam had to let him go.

Today, Sam and his brother don't speak to each other, even at family gatherings. Sam learned his lesson the hard way: don't hire anyone you can't fire!

EMPLOYEE EVALUATION

As we've discussed, many business owners fail to tell employees what is expected of them. Yet, in order to do a good job, employees need to know what a good job is. Then, they need to know how they measure up. Let's explore some ways to accomplish this.

Creating Job Descriptions and Personality Profiles

Once you recognize the importance of having perform-ance measurements, how do you go about creating them?

You start by creating a job description for each posi-tion. This is important not only for current employees, but for future hires and promotions. After all, you can't hire someone to fill a position until you define what that position is. Many small business owners tend to focus on the larger picture, and that's a good thing. In this case, however, detail is necessary. A good job description addresses all of the following:

- A detailed summary of the employee's specific tasks.
- The expected results, quantified as much as possible.
- The amount of authority and responsibility the position entails.
- The employee's manager (i.e., the reporting structure).

If the position entails multiple activities—as most do—prioritize them. Why? Because you can use the job description as a checklist as you evaluate candidates for an open position. You can't realistically expect one candidate to rate A+ in every area. By prioritizing activities, you can identify which candidate has the key skills you require. (If you hold out for someone who is outstanding in every area, you will never get around to actually hiring someone. And once you do hire someone, keep these priorities in mind as you measure his or her performance, giving most weight to the most important job activities.)

In addition to the job description, create a personality profile for the position. What personality traits are necessary to achieving success? An attention to detail? A broader vision? The ability to think quickly under pressure? One way to do this is to analyze the traits of current employees who are successfully performing the same type of work. They have the winning traits you seek! Remember, skills can be learned, but personality traits are something we are born with. Since they are an integral part of the candidate's makeup, make sure they'll work for you and not against you.

Here's an essential component that's often overlooked in the hiring process: detail your company's code of beliefs and values—and match them against your candidates' beliefs and values. During the interview process, don't just explore a candidate's work experience, probe his or her values. Ask situational questions that reveal the candidate's ethical position. For example, if a customer mistakenly overpaid, how would the candidate respond? If a candidate has the skills, work experience, and personality traits but doesn't hold the same values, don't make the hire! Chances are, it won't work out.

PRO members acknowledge that hiring is a painful process that takes them away from their daily business activities. Creating job descriptions and personality profiles also takes work and time. But once the work is done, it eases the hiring process tremendously. It also ensures that, rather than making poor decisions, you'll enhance your company's human assets. Each new hire is an opportunity to improve your organization.

When it comes to hiring, be like a good carpenter—measure twice, cut once.

Evaluation Methods

Most PRO members do not look forward to conducting annual performance evaluations. Nevertheless, nearly all are scrupulous in doing so—it's to everyone's benefit, employer and employees.

As I've previously said, most people want to do a good job. It's management's job to define what that good job is and to let employees know if they're on track. If you're not willing to do this, your employees can't deliver an optimum performance. You then risk alienating them down the road.

Think evaluations are only important in big companies? Wrong! They're especially important in small ones, because employees tend to have varied responsibilities. They need to know which ones to treat as priorities.

Companies use a range of evaluation formats. In a conventional evaluation, both the manager and employee are asked to critique the employee's performance, generally by completing evaluation forms. In comparing responses, it immediately becomes clear if they're on the same track. If there are huge differences in their perspectives, communication is not taking place. Generally speaking, if employees know what is expected of them, they know how they're doing. And that goes for managers and bosses, too.

Remember, the objective of all evaluations is not to criticize or defend, but to discover constructive ways to improve performance. The idea is not only to identify an employee's weak areas, but to develop a course of remediation (e.g., obtaining additional training or purchasing updated equipment). It is the employer's responsibility to track down solutions, involving the HR department if necessary. (In addition, this is the time to initiate progressive discipline if so required, and to create a schedule for future reviews—see the section "Truth or Consequences" on page 140.)

In addition to the conventional evaluation format, "360-degree" evaluations are popular with PRO members. The manager evaluates the employee's performance, while the employee reviews the manager's performance as it pertains to his job. Is the employee getting the training, guidance, and communication he needs? What can the manager do to help the employee perform at a higher level?

Yet another evaluation format is team evaluations. Members of a team who work together side by side have the opportunity to evaluate—constructively and anonymously—their fellow members' performance. Are team members supportive of one another's efforts? Is everyone carrying their share of the load? Does someone need training in a specific area? Team evaluations harness a very powerful motivational tool: namely, peer pressure. But it is important to make this a constructive, not destructive, exercise.

You have your choice of evaluation formats, so choose the type that best fits your work environment and company culture. The important thing is to make performance evaluations a regular and expected event. After all, you want to continually improve performance.

Evaluation vs. Valuation

There's a very big difference between evaluation and valuation—far more than just an "e."

Evaluation concerns job performance. An employee evaluation is a mutual dialogue between employer and employee. Has the employee achieved his or her goals? Valuation, on the other hand, is the monetary discussion concerning what that performance is worth.

Most PRO members have learned to separate an employee's evaluation from valuation by a period of one to two weeks. The evaluation, of course, comes first. Why?

Because if you combine the two into a single discussion, the employee will only want to hear about the raise she is going to get. She'll tune out of the rest of the discussion—the important part.

In an evaluation, you have the opportunity to tell your employee what your expectations are. You can discuss areas that need strengthening and how to get the necessary skills. It's your opportunity to make sure you're both on the same wavelength, to improve future performance, and to identify needed training.

Once the evaluation has taken place, the employee is in a better position to understand the valuation discussion. Of course, except in cases of a promotion or increase in responsibility, performance always comes before a pay increase.

Valuation is based on many factors, including company finances, what the position is worth to the company, and, of course, performance. The valuation discussion can set an incentive for the employee to achieve the goals you discussed during the evaluation. It can help realize priorities and may change behavior. Money talks—that's why you have to get your employees to listen first.

TERMINATIONS

As we discussed back in chapter 3, most small business owners are reluctant to terminate employees. But when training, mentoring, and coaching fails, termination is the last resort. It's not fair to keep an employee in a situation beyond his scope. It's not fair to the coworkers who have to pick up his slack. It's not fair to the company paying his salary. Nor is it fair to the employee, who is better served in a position where he can make a real contribution.

Let's examine the necessity of terminating underperformers and how to do it with professionalism and grace.

Truth or Consequences

In order for performance evaluations to be effective, they have to have teeth. You have to be ready to follow through with consequences—even if that means terminating a long-time employee.

Back in chapter 2, we talked about giving non-performers a "transfer" off your bus. We talked about how difficult it is to do. Well, it hasn't gotten any easier in the intervening chapters, but hopefully now you are more convinced of its necessity.

Enforcing consequences—probation, termination—is the only way to root out poor performance. One of the benefits of regular performance evaluations is that neither you nor your employees are caught by surprise.

If an employee's performance is under par, putting him on probation is a way to provide fair warning. Be very specific: tell your employee where his performance is lacking and what he must do to improve. Document it in writing, and schedule a follow-up evaluation several weeks down the road.

This is your employee's opportunity to change his behavior. It is also your opportunity to protect yourself from a wrongful termination lawsuit. The employee's performance—and your communications regarding it— must be documented each step of the way.

If the employee does not improve his performance in a tangible way, you must be ready to proceed with termination. Over the years, reluctant PRO members have found all kinds of reasons not to terminate employees, like "I'll do it after our busy season" or "But I have no one to replace him with!" These may be perfectly legitimate reasons, but it's also like saying the dog ate your homework. Nobody's buying it. And no one will buy your employee evaluations unless they know you'll stand behind them.

The 20% Rule

One of our PRO members, Kevin, has an interesting theory he calls "The 20% Rule." According to the 20% Rule, most employee populations fit this demographic:

- 20% are good/great performers
- 20% are poor performers
- 60% are average performers

Now think about that 60 percent majority. How can you improve the performance of these employees? According to Kevin's theory, how you handle "bad" employees will determine the future behavior of average performers.

If you tolerate mediocrity, then your average employees will start underperforming, too. And why shouldn't they? There are no consequences for slacking off.

If, on the other hand, you refuse to tolerate poor performance, your average employees will pick up the pace. When Kevin started terminating his poorly performing employees, productivity soared!

Yes, some of it was driven by fear, but such terminations also boost morale among good workers. It sends the message that you know who's getting the work done—and that it matters.

INCENTIVES/COMPENSATION

What do employees really want? Incentives and compensation are important to motivating employees, but don't assume it always comes down to dollars. When it comes to inspiring your employees, it takes more than a paycheck. Here are some creative ways to motivate your people.

Bah Humbug! Doing Away with the Christmas Bonus

Very few PRO members can be called Scrooges. However, every November—without fail—conversation turns to the issue of the Christmas bonus.

Most PRO members are happy to share the wealth, but they're not at all happy with traditional Christmas bonuses. Why? Because an employee who receives annual

Christmas bonuses comes to consider it part of his salary. He sees it as his due, and it goes largely unappreciated.

That's why many PRO members have shifted away from the Christmas bonus and towards an incentive-based bonus. A Christmas bonus doesn't spur performance...an incentive bonus does. And, really, isn't that the purpose of any reward system?

Ah, but shifting away from the revered Christmas bonus is a delicate business. Here are some tips for making a successful transition:

- Design a viable incentive plan that includes individual employee objectives and concrete performance measurements.
- Introduce your incentive plan at the beginning of a new year—never in October or November! You want your employees to view this as an improvement, not a takeaway. Be sure to position it as such.
- Plan to pay bonuses more than once a year—perhaps biannually or quarterly. For one thing, it lets employees know how they're doing and allows them to adjust their performance along the way. For another, it keeps employee motivation high, because the next payout is never out of view. And last of all, it may prevent your employees from going into debt, hoping their year-end bonus will bail them out.

Do you find yourself resisting this idea? Remember, you are not taking anything away. If the incentive system works, it may actually end up costing you more. Investing in your company's future—and making tough financial decisions—is essential to your long-term survival. Don't think merely in terms of this year and next year. Look further down the road.

Benevolent dictator types (see page 25) are comfortable with the Christmas bonus because it keeps them in control. However, you can structure an incentive-based system in a way that keeps you in the driver's seat. For example, base 70 to 80 percent of the employee's bonus on measurable performance goals, and reserve 20 to 30 percent for management discretion. That gives you room to address intangibles that fall outside of the written criteria.

PRO member Bob, who owns a woodworking company, was very apprehensive when he replaced his traditional Christmas bonus with an incentive-based system. To his amazement, he found that his employees preferred being rewarded for their achievements. Since implementing the incentive bonus, he has virtually eliminated turnover—and that's a bonus he didn't foresee!

An important footnote: if you have a bad year and suspect there will be no bonus or very small ones, it's critical to start communicating it early on and to provide details so people understand the reasons. Otherwise, morale will plummet when your employees learn the bad news.

Using Unusual Incentives

People are different, and that includes your employees. What motivates one person won't do a thing for another. One of the benefits of small business is its flexibility. You have the flexibility to reward each employee individually, according to his or her personal hot buttons.

When it comes to incentives, most people assume that "cash is king." The consensus among PRO members is that recognition works even better. And offering personalized incentives is a wonderful form of recognition.

PRO members have come up with a number of creative incentives for their employees. Maybe some of these will work for you, too:

- If an employee has been working extra-long hours, send a thank-you bouquet or gift to his or her spouse. Thank the spouse for being a good sport about all that overtime. You'll get plenty of mileage from it.
- Keep the home fires burning. Promise a fabulous vacation in return for reaching a goal—and send the progress reports to your employee's home address. Let the spouse turn up the heat.
- Engage in "profit sharing." If your company reaches a certain goal each month, give everyone some kind of bonus. One of our members who owns a print shop does this. He reports that, as month's-end approaches, watching his employees hustle makes it worth every penny.
- In lieu of cash bonuses, offer tickets to sporting events or the theater, gourmet dinners, or weekend getaways—whatever gets your employees' juices flowing. Whether it's a visit to the day spa or a

favorite golf course, a personalized reward will make an employee feel special.

- The more creative, the better. One PRO member promised his office manager—who was building a new home—a high-end refrigerator if certain goals were met. It worked!
- Don't underestimate the power of an "employee of the month" campaign. Small things like a reserved parking space and special pin or paperweight may seem corny, but they're very effective.

Remember, the shorter the time frame between the promise and the reward, the more motivated your employees will be. A yearlong sales contest, for example, may backfire. If an employee starts off slow, he may give up and write off the year before the first quarter is over. For this reason, several shorter contests with smaller awards are preferable to one long one.

Golden Handcuffs: The Anecdote to Greener Pastures

You're undoubtedly familiar with noncompete, nondisclosure, and confidentially agreements. These are all good defensive tactics that keep former employees from making off with your accounts. However, a good offense will keep the defense off the field—and that's better yet. So, what positive steps can you take to keep your employees tied to you?

One answer is a pair of golden handcuffs. Simply stated, it is a financial reward, one that is carefully structured so that if the employee leaves the company, it translates to a financial loss. If they stay, they gain. If they leave, they have pain.

PRO members have designed various types of golden handcuffs, custom fitted for each wearer. They can be very simple or extremely complex.

For example, Brian designed a simple plan for his key saleswoman. He pays the cost of leasing a car. However, the lease is in her name, and she is under obligation to pay it. Should she leave his employment, the unpaid portion becomes her responsibility. Another PRO member uses this same concept—only instead of a car, he's footing the bill for his manager's MBA tuition.

Other PRO members use more complex programs, including deferred compensation and salary continuation programs. These include secular trusts, rabbi trusts, and straightforward deferred compensation/disability agreements—all employer/employee agreements stipulating some continued compensation upon attainment of retirement (or other special conditions, such as disability). Some are funded with current dollars; others are not. In each case, the employer agrees to take on a financial obligation if the employee fulfills his part of the agreement. Should the employee leave before the agreed-upon time, he forfeits all or some of the benefits.

Still other PRO members encourage key employees to feel like equity participants by either giving them or allowing them to purchase (perhaps at a discount) market equity stock in the company.

It should be noted that many business owners do not like to create minority shareholders. Instead, they create a phantom stock program. The employee is not an actual owner. The payout occurs when a dividend is declared, if the company is sold, or at an agreed-upon retirement date. Then employees receive proceeds in percentage to their phantom position.

Because golden handcuffs tend to be technical in nature, it's important to develop them with the help of your attorney and accountant as well as the employee. Remember, whatever shape they take, they must be of great value to the employee. Pain of loss occurs only when something important hangs in the balance.

The Golden Hello

As you might presume, the golden hello is like golden handcuffs—except it is a hiring incentive.

For example, after an extensive search, Ron found the perfect second-in-command last June. The candidate met every one of Ron's extensive criteria. There was only one problem: the candidate wanted to stay with his current employer until the end of the year so he could collect his $25,000 year-end bonus.

Rather than lose him, Ron structured an irresistible golden hello—a $10,000 signing bonus after his first day of work, followed by a $15,000 bonus after ninety days on the job. It was compelling enough to bring the candidate aboard.

The popularity of the golden hello tends to rise and wane with the job market. When the market is soft, you don't see them as often. However, regardless of the job market, golden candidates are hard to come by. If you find the right person, you might want to extend a golden hello.

Wowing Your Employees

The best way to keep your employees (and keep them productive) is to keep them happy—to wow them, if you will. But there is no single, magical ingredient for wowing employees. Rather, it is a combination of ingredients. According to PRO members, these include:

- Offering appropriate incentives.
- Treating employees fairly (this includes communicating expectations).
- Providing recognition.
- Asking for input.
- Creating a pleasant, comfortable work environment.
- Hiring people who share your values and goals.

And here's one more thing you can do: add an element of fun. Make your people look forward to coming to work. Forming a golf or softball league, treating your staff to ice cream socials, and even posting a joke of the day are all ways to add fun and build camaraderie.

You can even turn negatives into positives this way. For example, when one PRO member needed to cut costs, he created a "Buck-a-Day" contest, inviting employees to share ideas for economizing in return for wacky prizes. He used posters, PA announcements, and silly props to capture their imagination. For several weeks, employees had no idea what they'd find when they stepped through the door each morning. This created a collective sense of anticipation—and buy-in for his campaign.

You don't have to spend a fortune to wow your employees. Just get the right components in place, and add some imagination.

The Elevator Test

I mentioned earlier that a complicated incentive formula is in itself a disincentive. Who wants to work for a company that can't tell you how and how much it will pay you?

This is a train wreck in the making. If employees don't understand how they are compensated, you can't effectively tie performance to compensation, leading to confused, underperforming workers. And it's only a matter of time before someone becomes disgruntled because his or her pay falls short of expectations.

How do you evaluate the simplicity of your compensation formula? Submit it to the "elevator test." Try explaining your formula in the time it takes to ride an elevator from the top floor down. Can't do it? Then elevate your thinking—and simplify and redefine your compensation formula.

The Employee Benefits Report Card

Your employee benefits are an important—and expensive!—part of your compensation package. Yet many employees don't fully appreciate them. One recent HR study concluded that employees underrate the cost of their benefits by about 20 percent—when in fact benefits generally equal 15 to 40 percent of wages.

What can you do to raise your employees' benefits IQ? For starters, make sure all your benefit plans and choices are communicated on a regular basis in a format that is easy to understand. Your insurance carrier or agent should provide clear written summaries of coverage (and annual enrollment meetings, if warranted). If you have an employee handbook (and it's a good idea), it should include an explanation of vacation days, sick days, and holidays, etc.

Another device many PRO members use is the annual "Employee Benefits Report Card." This statement—personalized for each employee—not only lists every conceivable benefit he or she receives, but its monetary value. Here, employees can appreciate the worth of their vacation time, health insurance, workers' comp, and more. You can even remind them of the communal benefits they receive, such as free coffee and pizza parties.

Need help getting started? See the sample statement provided by one of our PRO members. If you don't have the time or resources to compile these yourself, you can hire an HR service firm to do it for you.

EMPLOYEE BENEFIT AND COMPENSATION STATEMENT
YEAR ENDING DECEMBER 31, 2003

We know you'll be interested in learning the total amount of your compensation for the past year, including your salary and all fringe benefits we paid on your behalf.

2003 Earnings

Salary (37.5 hours/per week)	$36,848.15
Paid Vacation	$2,417.33
Paid Sick Days	$1,434.80
Paid Holidays	$3,624.26
Paid Funeral Leave	$0.00
Paid Jury Duty	$0.00
Paid Personal Days	*$0.00*
Total W-2 Earnings	$44,324.54
Benefits	
Medical, Life & Disability Insurance	$2,025.77
FICA (company share)	$2,653.07
Unemployment Ins.	$825.00
Workers' Compensation Insurance	$225.83
Contribution to Retirement Plan	$3,684.81
Matching 401(K) Plan Contribution	$924.54
Continuing Professional Education Seminars	$1,297.50
Automobile/Mileage Reimbursement	*$0.00*
Total Benefits	$11,636.52
Total Earnings & Benefits	$55,961.06
% of Benefits of Earnings	21%

In addition, you received the following company-paid benefits, which are shared among all employees:

Free coffee & tea

Quarterly staff luncheons

Annual Christmas party

Holiday ham or turkey

Use of company long distance phone service

Use of company Internet service

Free parking/van pooling

Payroll deduction options (IRA, savings bonds, voluntary life insurance, etc.)

The above benefits represent our best estimates, based on actual salary shown. These figures do not represent any obligation on our part beyond items already paid or incurred.

How to Minimize Turnover

Has this ever happened to you? You recruit a highly qualified person for a key position. You think everything is fine, but within the first year, she gives her notice. What a blow! Your ask yourself, *What went wrong?* More important, how can you keep this from happening again?

A number of PRO members have had the same experience. As a result, they have developed some strategies for minimizing turnover, especially when hiring for key positions. Perhaps you will find their experiences useful.

Let's start with Mark, a professional recruiter. Mark won't recommend a candidate to a client unless the candidate meets at least two of the following criteria:

1. *Location*—The job site (and commute) must be agreeable to the candidate.
2. *Compensation*—The candidate must be fully satisfied with the proposed compensation, as well as the terms for future compensation.
3. *Position*—The candidate must fully understand the job, its responsibilities, and authority—and must find them completely agreeable.

In Mark's experience, a candidate who accepts a position purely for compensation will not stay long. That's why it's important to achieve consensus in more than one area.

Then there's Lois, who believes firmly in the value of exit interviews. She asserts they are your rare chance to see things through an employee's eyes. You'll not only find out what went wrong, but learn some interesting things about your organization.

Ideally, says Lois, wait thirty days after the employee leaves before conducting the interview. For one thing, it allows the dust to settle and heated emotions to cool. You're more likely to receive candid information.

For another, as time passes, an employee may find that the grass isn't actually greener on the other side. If you separate on good terms, it's possible that employee might want to come back. If it's a good employee, it's often advantageous to rehire her. She's a known entity, and now she has a new appreciation of your company's strengths and benefits.

The smart small business owner takes pains to minimize turnover by hiring wisely. Don't hire on the basis of skills alone. Make sure you're compatible in terms of job expectations, location, and compensation—as well as company culture, beliefs, values, and personality traits. A good sense of humor goes a long way, too.

No one likes losing good employees. But as PRO member Roger notes, when it does occur, try to view it as an opportunity—an opportunity to enhance your talent pool and hire someone even better.

Think of your company like a racecar. In the end, it's all about performance. To operate at peak efficiency, you need to have the right parts—in other words, staff—perfectly positioned in just the right places. Ongoing tune-ups—evaluations, terminations, and recruiting efforts—are essential to keep the gears turning smoothly. And you need high-octane fuel—that is, powerful incentives—to keep that engine in tip-top shape.

CHAPTER SIX

HUMAN ASSETS

You can't grow your company all by yourself. Employees are critical to a company's success. This is especially true in small companies, where every employee's contribution makes a tangible difference.

Therefore, don't view recruiting as a chore, but an opportunity to enhance the organization. Cultivate good morale, teamwork, and open communication. Take great care to nip personnel problems in the bud. Human assets are your most valuable assets and should be treated as such.

RECRUITING

Attracting top performers begins with a concentrated recruiting effort. Don't limit yourself to the conventional methods that your competitors use. And don't wait until you have an urgent position to fill to build your strategy. Here are some creative recruiting ideas that you can start using right now.

The 24/7/365 Recruiting Program

Finding qualified candidates is one of the most pressing challenges faced by business owners. You know they are out there—but where?

The best recruiting approach is a long-term approach, what we at PRO call the "24/7/365 Recruiting Program." This means keeping your eyes open at all times—even when you're not actively hiring. PRO members utilize a number of smart strategies for round-the-clock recruiting. Here's the top ten:

Smart Strategies for 25/7/265 Recruiting

1. Pretend that you're building your own major league baseball team, complete with a farm system. Keep an ongoing list of impact players you meet during the course of business. You'll be ready when it's time to make a trade or hire a free agent.

2. Always keep your business card handy. When you meet someone you like, don't be bashful: give her your card and tell her outright that you want to discuss a job opportunity. When you see someone with the right attitude, grab her!

3. Keep your eyes open at trade shows, not-for-profit boards, even at church. In these environments, you have the opportunity to observe a potential

---

candidate's work ethic, communication skills, and speed of learning...without an interview!

4. When calling on customers or prospects, take a look at their sign-in book—it's a goldmine. You may find dozens of experienced sales reps who already know your client or target market.

5. Take advantage of the Internet. Many websites, such as Monster.com, list both openings and resumes. The cost to list a position is not expensive, and you can include more details than in a classified ad. (You can also reference your own website on business cards and promotional materials. Sharing your company's objectives and attitudes will help draw the kind of candidates you want.)

6. Research your market by visiting the websites of your competition or firms that resemble yours in terms of distribution or needed employee skill sets. Sometimes companies will list their employees on their sites, literally identifying potential candidates for you.

7. Ask your employees if they can recommend a good candidate. They know your work ethic and culture, and they won't recommend anyone they don't want to work with. Consider offering a finder's fee for successful hires.

8. Ask your customers and vendors. Because they are familiar with your company, they can suggest people who may fit in well. Describe the position and job requirements, as well as the "soft" ingredients you're seeking.

9. Ask your customers for the names of outstanding sales and service people. You may even query potential customers if you have established enough rapport with them. (This also offers you the opportunity to talk about your company's core values—and that may even land the account.)

10. Reconsider traditional hiring techniques. Place ads in the classifieds, giving special consideration to trade journals, or hire a recruiter. Think recruiters are expensive? When you factor in all the direct/indirect costs of advertising, screening, and interviewing, a good recruiter may be a bargain.

Finding qualified people is not as complicated as you may think. Even if you're not hiring today, start practicing the 24/7/365 approach and you'll always have a place to begin.

CASE STUDY: JOE

Joe, who owns a small factory, frequently eats lunch at a sandwich shop across the street from his facility.

Several years ago, Joe became impressed by one of the counter clerks at the luncheonette. This young man took his job very seriously and was careful to fix Joe's sandwich just the way he liked it.

It occurred to Joe that he would like to have more employees like that working in his factory. Then it occurred to Joe that, instead of finding someone like the counter clerk, he could hire the clerk himself.

As a courtesy, Joe asked the owner of the sandwich store if he would mind. As it turned out, the owner did not—the young man's wife was pregnant and they could use the bigger paycheck.

So Joe hired the counter clerk and both of them benefited. Wherever you are, it pays to keep your eyes open for talent!

Recruit Like You Market

One way to ease hiring challenges is to structure your recruiting program like you would a marketing program. If you have tough positions to fill, this can be especially helpful. In other words, make an effort to "sell" candidates on your company, just like you would sell them your products or services. For example:

- *Define your "Unique Selling Proposition"*—In this case, the emphasis is on your company's culture. Explain why people like working in your environment. Is it because of your open-office attitude? Your casual dress code? Is it because you're open to telecommuting? The free coffee? Or your employee appreciation parties? All of these things contribute to your recruiting USP.
- *Identify the Benefits*—In addition to compensation, do you offer the opportunity for internal advancement? Specialized training? The opportunity to

work in a cutting-edge industry? Be sure to promote the many benefits of working for your company.

- *Turn Negatives into Positives*—If you have a hard-to-fill spot, figure out why. Then try to extrapolate some unexpected advantages. For example, one PRO member couldn't find someone to work as a freight dispatcher because it was an unconventional, isolated position. Finally, he hit on a winning angle: "Tattoos Welcome!" which he advertised in college newspapers. There he found a surplus of willing, admittedly unconventional, candidates.

Is Your Website Soft and Fuzzy?

Your website isn't just a vehicle for attracting customers—it can also be used to attract new employees.

You have the space; use it to talk about your company and its employment opportunities. Here is the perfect place to describe your culture and value system, so you can attract like-minded job hunters. Many companies routinely post job openings on their website—something worth considering if you're often looking for help.

Remember, job hunters frequently use the Internet as a tool for identifying prospective employers. Look at your website from their eyes and make them want to work for you.

INTERVIEWING

A candidate's resume will tell you if she has the right qualifications. But an interview can tell you much more, like whether she has the right "soft skills" and how she will mesh with your company culture.

Many small business owners dislike interviewing and therefore fail to properly prepare for them. As a result, the process isn't revealing as it could be. Don't fall into this trap! Interviews are a rare opportunity to identify your next superstar and avoid hiring blunders. Here are some ways to make the most of them.

What Candidates Lie About

You don't believe everything you hear, do you? It is not uncommon for job applicants to exaggerate—and even lie—on their resumes and applications. But it may shock you just how prevalent this practice is.

One of our members, John, owns a security firm that performs background checks for corporate clients. According to John, 33 percent of the applicants he's vetted have made false claims to prospective employers. Another study puts that number at 54 percent—more than half of all job candidates!

So what are all these people lying about? Usually, it's one of two things: compensation or education.

It's easy to verify compensation: ask your applicants to bring their 1099 or W-2 form along on the interview. This is especially important in sales jobs. You can quickly see how successful—and truthful—someone is.

When it comes to education, you can do a couple of things. You can ask to see a diploma. You can order a professional background check. Or you can ask very specific questions about your candidate's studies and see if the answers ring true.

Performing background checks is a good idea, for all kinds of reasons. Our resident security expert, John, notes that one out of five candidates he's investigated has some kind of criminal record—something many fail to disclose on their application. While people have a right to a second chance, you have a right to that information. Why put your employees or company at risk?

Many small employers shun background checks, either because of the cost or because they want to maintain a warm, open environment. While admirable, in this day and age it may leave you vulnerable.

In addition, always check out a candidate's references and prior employers. Try to get past the HR department; it won't give you the kind of information you want. Always ask if there is "anyone else you can talk to." Ideally, you'd like to talk to your candidate's former manager and coworkers, as well as workers he managed. If you can get a dialogue going, you'll have a better sense of who your candidate really is.

Finally, don't hesitate to question what's on the resume. If someone claims to have boosted sales by 10 percent, ask her how she did it, step by step. If her claim is a lie, you'll want to know. And if it's true...well, you can benefit from that information, too!

Innovative Interviewing Techniques

The purpose of interviewing is to get an honest sense of the person in front of you. If you stick to the stock questions, you'll get stock answers. In order to discover the real individual, ask the unexpected. Throw a few curveballs.

Here are some the interesting techniques used by PRO members:

- *Don't start by doing all the talking.* Many employers ease into interviews by telling candidates all about their companies. The fact is you'll learn much more about your candidate if you launch right into your questions. First of all, if your candidate is on the ball, he'll already be able to demonstrate some knowledge of your company. (The Internet has made it very easy to perform such background research.) Second, if you don't provide cues regarding your priorities, your candidate can't parrot them and will have to volunteer his own ideas. Finally, telling your candidate "I'm interested in *you*" is a great way to sell him on your company.

- *Ask open-ended questions, ones that can't be answered yes or no.* Follow each one with another open-ended question. This will force your candidate to give longer, more thoughtful responses. Need some ideas? PRO members have compiled a list of forty-eight open-ended questions (see the following).

- *Make the candidate do the questioning.* Before a second or third interview, ask your candidate to submit ten questions about the company. The questions will reveal why he wants the job. For the money? The satisfaction? Or the free coffee?

If it becomes clear at any time that a candidate is not for you, cut the interview short. It doesn't make sense to go through the motions for the sake of being polite. Why waste your time—or the candidate's?

48 OPEN-ENDED INTERVIEWING QUESTIONS

1. Describe a time in your last job when you encountered obstacles while you were in pursuit of a goal. What happened?
2. We have all failed to meet company quota at one time or another. When you don't meet those goals, how do you handle it?
3. Tell me about the most difficult sale you ever made.
4. How would your customers describe you?
5. In what areas do you typically have the least amount of patience at work?
6. How would you grade your ability to communicate with upper-level management, customers, and peers?
7. Tell me about a time when you and your previous boss disagreed but you still found a way to get your point across.
8. In your opinion, what does it take to be a "success"?
9. What kinds of customers upset you? How do you deal with them?
10. How do you handle rejection?
11. What are three keys to successful telephone sales?

12. What could your past employers count on you for, without fail?

13. Give me two examples of things you've done in previous jobs that demonstrate your willingness to work hard.

14. How do you define your closing style?

15. Jobs have pros and cons. What do you see as the pros and cons of selling?

16. How motivated are you by money?

17. What does growth in the job mean to you?

18. How do you approach your work from the standpoint of balancing your career and your personal life?

19. Tell me about a time when you turned an occasional buyer into a regular buyer.

20. What should a salesperson know about each customer?

21. How do you go about establishing rapport with a prospect?

22. What kind of hours do you typically work?

23. Give me two examples of decisions you had to make on your last job.

24. What two or three things are important to you in a job?

25. Of all the work you have done, where have you been the most successful?

26. Do you prefer to speak with someone or send a memo or an email?

27. Think of something that you consider a failure in your career. What did you learn from it?

28. What is the most important feature to you in a job?
29. What do you do when things are slow at work?
30. How do you like to be managed?
31. How do you know you are doing a good job?
32. How do you manage your paperwork when you would rather be selling?
33. Selling can be stressful. How do you manage stress?
34. Tell me about a time when you were making a sales call and put your foot in your mouth.
35. What two adjectives best describe you?
36. What were (or are) the biggest pressures on your last (or present) job?
37. What are some of the things your supervisor did that you disliked?
38. What are some of the basic factors that motivate you in your work?
39. Tell me about the most unusual objection you ever got and how you handled it.
40. Tell me about a sale you lost that really hurt.
41. What causes you to lose your temper?
42. Tell me about a time when, rather than following instructions, you went about a task in your own way. What happened?
43. What two or three things are important to you in a job?
44. What is the most intellectually challenging thing you are looking for in a job, and why?
45. What are your most important long-term goals?
46. How would you react if you were asked to fill in

for someone who has different, even lower-level, responsibilities?

47. At what times do you have trouble communicating with people?

48. How do you prioritize your time?

The Importance of Humor

Humor has an important role in the workplace. Studies demonstrate that people who have fun at work are more creative, productive, and get along better with coworkers. As we discussed, creating a fun environment also helps attract and retain employees.

So the other side of the equation is to hire candidates who have a demonstrated sense of humor. Southwest Airlines is famous for hiring "people-people." Look at the company's job qualifications—you'll find "a sense of humor" up there on the company's short list. Think about it. When flights are delayed, cancelled, or overbooked, a smile and a touch of humor can go a long way toward soothing ruffled customers.

When you're interviewing, ask outright how the candidate has used humor as a workplace tool—and if so, to give an example. And, of course, throughout the interview itself, see if he employs humor as a way to win you over.

CASE STUDY: TERRY

No matter how good your company is, you will occasionally have to deal with irate customers. Terry uses humor to mend those fences.

When an order goes out incorrectly, Terry will personally call the customer and give them this line: "To err is human, to forgive is divine. I'm sorry we gave you the opportunity to demonstrate your divinity!"

STAYING OUT OF TROUBLE

Many small business owners shy away from negative performance reviews because they want to be nice. But in the long run, being honest is the nicer thing to do. For one thing, the employer's silence deprives employees of the opportunity to improve. For another, that silence may land the employer in hot water if, somewhere down the road, he terminates an underperformer.

When it comes to staying out of trouble, communication is the key. Let's examine some techniques for communicating with employees in an honest, professional manner, while protecting your company from future legal headaches.

Nice Guys End Up in Lawsuits

Earlier, we discussed the necessity of providing honest employee evaluations. We talked about the need to document employee performance and provide fair warning by using probation. This is not just a fair way to treat your employees—it's the way to protect yourself from wrongful termination lawsuits.

If you're "too nice" to tell an employee that he is underperforming on the job, you may just end up telling him in court someday. Nice guys do finish last sometimes. Don't be so nice that you jeopardize—or compromise—your company.

It's never too late to update or start enforcing employment policies. Even if you haven't done a good job up to now, you can make changes going forward (and the sooner you do, the better).

Enforce your other policies as well, especially those regarding absenteeism, tardiness, etc. Make sure they are clearly communicated in writing. Documentation is the key. Most employees appreciate honest communication.

Remember, if you have been overlooking the behavior of a few slackers, you are discriminating against your good employees. And that's not so nice, is it?

The Benefit of Exit Interviews

Exit interviews, as mentioned earlier, give you the rare opportunity to learn how your employees really think. Because your exiting employee has nothing to lose, chances are she will offer honest feedback.

What's good about working for your company? What's bad? This is your chance to see things the way your employees do and correct any problems you may uncover. If you have morale or attitude troubles brewing, this is an excellent way to discover them.

Of course, during any given interview, you are only hearing what one employee has to say...and a possibly unhappy employee at that. Needless to say, all comments should be taken with a grain of salt. However, if you start hearing common refrains, you'll know the subject is worthy of your attention.

If possible, wait thirty days before conducting the interview. By then, the glory of the new position might have dimmed a bit. Similarly, a disgruntled ex-employee may no longer be so angry. Allowing a cooling-off period gives employees a chance to be more objective in their final assessment.

In addition, a cordial exit interview gives you the opportunity to end the relationship on a positive note. You do not want disgruntled ex-employees badmouthing you throughout the industry. By behaving professionally, you'll remind the employee to behave professionally, too—and that can indeed keep you out of trouble.

How to Handle Severance Issues: The Severance Release

Severance can be a tricky thing. Today, all employers must be sensitive to the possible perception of discrimination, whether age, gender, race, or something else is at issue. It is not particularly difficult for a disgruntled employee to put together a bias suit, which (even if it's preposterous) can spell big headaches for an employer.

A verbal agreement is not enough. The best protection is a written, signed severance agreement. To get an employee to sign such an agreement, you may wish to offer a severance package. You agree to pay the employee X amount of money over X amount of time, and in return, the employee agrees to release you from any accusations of bias. The dollar amount of the severance should be fair and equitable. You should feel good about giving it.

You will find a sample severance agreement to follow. Of course, you'll want to have your own attorney review and adapt it as necessary.

How do severance agreements work? Once the employee signs the agreement, he has a fixed number of days in which to recant. To ensure compliance, withhold the first payment until after the employee's time to recant is up.

It may be a good idea to spread the payments out over time to discourage your ex-employees from having a change of heart and from violating any possible noncompete and nonsolicitation agreements they have entered into.

SAMPLE RELEASE AND WAIVER AGREEMENT

This Agreement is between you, _____ (for yourself, your spouse, and your agents and attorneys), and ABC Corporation, including its officers, agents, attorneys, and its successors (jointly called "ABC Corp.").

By entering into this Agreement, neither you nor ABC Corp. admits any wrongdoing.

In this Agreement, in exchange for the payments and benefits described in paragraph 10, you are waiving and

---

releasing all claims and causes of action you may have against ABC Corp. on the day you sign this Agreement that arise out of your employment, except as may be necessary to enforce the provisions of this Agreement.

The claims and causes of action you are releasing and waiving include, but are not limited to, any and all claims and causes of action that ABC Corp.:

Has violated public policy, its personnel policies, handbooks, or any contract of employment between you and it; or

Has discriminated against you on the basis of age (or any claim or right arising under the Age Discrimination in Employment Act of 1967), race, color, sex, national origin, ancestry, disability, religion, sexual orientation, marital status, parental status, source of income, entitlement to benefits, or any union activities in violation of local (city and/or county), state or federal regulations; or

Has defamed you, invaded your privacy, or inflicted emotional distress on you.

You also agree that you have been paid for all hours worked, have not suffered any on-the-job injury for which you have not already filed a claim, and have received all the sick and vacation pay you were owed.

You also agree that:

You are entering into this Agreement knowingly and voluntarily;

You have been advised by ABC Corp. to consult an attorney;

You agree this Agreement is written in a manner

calculated to be understood by you, and you understand all the terms of this Agreement;

You have full knowledge of the legal consequences of this Agreement;

You have been provided a period of twenty-one (21) days within which to consider this Agreement;

Following the execution of this Agreement, you will have a period of seven (7) days to revoke it, and it shall not become effective or enforceable until the revocation period has expired;

In addition to the waiver and release by you of all other claims, this Agreement results in the waiver and release by you of all claims arising under the Age Discrimination in Employment Act of 1967, 29 U.S. C. 621 *et seq.* ("ADEA");

In exchange for the waiver and release by you of all ADEA claims, you are receiving consideration in addition to anything of value to which you already are entitled to as a result of your employment with ABC Corp. and you are not otherwise entitled to the payments or benefits described in paragraph 10; and

You waive any and all rights to reinstate with ABC Corp. and agree never to seek work with ABC Corp. in the future.

The provisions of this Agreement are severable, and if any part of it is found to be non-enforceable, the other paragraphs shall remain fully valid and enforceable. This Agreement shall survive the termination of any arrangements contained herein. Any failure of ABC Corp. to enforce a provision of this Agreement shall not be construed as a waiver of ABC Corp. of the right to do so.

This Agreement is confidential between you and ABC Corp., and you shall not disclose the existence of this Agreement and/or its contents to any individual, entity, or otherwise.

After you sign this Agreement, you will have seven (7) days to revoke it. If you want to revoke it, you must deliver a written revocation to _____ for receipt within seven (7) days of this Agreement. In the event you revoke this Agreement or you do not sign this Agreement, you will only be given that which you have already received from ABC Corp., this Agreement shall be null and void, and neither party shall have any obligation under this Agreement.

If you sign and do not revoke this Agreement, ABC Corp. shall provide you with additional severance pay, less applicable deductions, for a net total of _____ dollars ($ _____).

Signed:

_____

Date

_____

ABC Corp.   Date

Documenting Progressive Discipline

"I like to maintain a family feel in my company." I hear that often from PRO members, particularly in defense of their lack of rules and policies. That's okay. Many of us share the same inclination.

After all, a warm, informal atmosphere can lead to a good we're-all-in-this-together work environment. In fact, it may be one reason why your employees choose to work for you rather than a huge corporate employer.

But if you're putting your company at risk because of your ideal of a "family atmosphere," sooner or later you may wind up in big trouble. Things change. People change. And that can include your employees.

That's why it is essential to document your employment performance and attitude policies in writing. You must have some kind of employee handbook. It should specify all unacceptable behaviors (such as excessive tardiness and absenteeism) and spell out any actions (such as theft) that will result in immediate termination. It should also specify your sexual discrimination policy, as well as holidays and your vacation policy.

I hope you'll never need to refer to this information. But if a situation arises, you have a standard to follow, plus documented support for the consequences you impose.

The same thing goes for performance reviews. Document all reviews in writing. Use the technique of progressive discipline discussed earlier in this chapter, and be sure to document it. If you are going to fire someone, proof that you provided notice (e.g., gave her a warning or placed her on probation) could keep you on the winning side of a wrongful termination lawsuit.

Whenever you provide an employee with some kind of documentation—whether an employee handbook or a warning—have the employee sign a receipt, indicating he has received and understood the document.

You can still maintain a family feel while also maintaining clear expectations and protecting your company. When it doubt, document it. You'll never regret documenting something that never actually gets used. But believe me, if you fail to document a situation and it comes back to haunt you, you'll be kicking yourself for years to come.

CUTBACKS, LAYOFFS, AND OUTPLACEMENT

No one enjoys making cutbacks in staff, but sometimes it's absolutely necessary. However, there is a right way and wrong way to let people go. PRO members have developed some unconventional strategies that have worked for them. Maybe they'll work for you, too.

Overcut—The Kindest Cut

Employee cutbacks are terribly hard...on you, on the affected employees, and on those employees who remain. Unfortunately, in certain situations, cutbacks and layoffs are necessary to the company's survival.

No one enjoys letting workers go. And everyone recognizes that when cutbacks occur, morale takes a nosedive. Those employees who survive the first round of cutbacks report to work each day with one thought on their minds: *Am I next?*

So what's the kindest, least damaging way to implement cutbacks? PRO members have tried various approaches over the years. What we have discovered may surprise you.

Take PRO member Paul, for example. Paul's company manufactures luggage. Following the 9/11 attacks, his business—like the entire travel industry—plummeted.

Unwilling to lay off one more employee than necessary, he implemented some very modest cutbacks. He soon found it wasn't enough. He had to a second round of layoffs, followed by a third.

His employees were terrified. Morale continued to plunge, followed by productivity and quality, in a vicious downward spiral.

Contrast that with Samantha, who owns a large travel agency. Her company was also devastated by 9/11. However, rather than introduce a series of small, ineffective layoffs, she made the decision to make one huge cutback—to overcut.

It sounds drastic, but in doing so, she put herself in a position where she could soon begin calling employees back to work. And what a morale builder that was!

Should you tell your employees you're overcutting? No! It doesn't serve employees to know that they've been laid off to protect company morale and productivity. Besides, you don't know for sure if or when you'll call them back. What's the value of offering false hope?

Overcutting achieves two purposes. For one thing, it immediately reduces your operating expenses. For another, it helps alleviate the fear of those employees left standing, which allows business to continue on a more normal basis. According to the consensus of PRO members, overcuts are the kindest cuts.

The Politically Correct Way to Get Rid of a Political Problem

So you made the mistake of hiring someone you know, and he or she is not working out. What do you do now? Many PRO members have made this mistake, but one of them came up with a clever win/win solution.

Against his better judgment, PRO member Bill found himself hiring his general manager's son. The son knew the business, but was disorganized and unproductive. Other employees resented having to pick up the slack. Meanwhile, the son was increasingly dissatisfied because he wasn't getting the promotions he wanted. The PRO member valued his general manager. If he fired the son, he would alienate the father, too.

Rather than approach either father or son, Bill went outside the company for his solution. He hired a recruiter to lure the problem employee away. It worked! The PRO member was happy to pay the recruiter's fee, the employee was happy to get a new job, and the general manager never knew the difference. When you play your cards right, everybody wins.

IDEAS FOR YOUR BENEFIT PROGRAM

As we discussed earlier, benefits are important to employees and serve as a powerful motivational tool. Unfortunately, good benefits are expensive. Don't pay a penny more than you need to! When it comes to benefits, always be receptive to cost-cutting alternatives that don't compromise quality—like these.

Cutting Health Insurance Costs (Without Cutting Benefits)

Health insurance costs are undoubtedly a huge chunk of your expenses, and it doesn't appear that relief is in sight. At the same time, health insurance remains among the most valued of all employee benefits.

If you haven't already, you owe it to yourself to investigate alternative health plans. I'm not talking about changing insurance carriers or switching to a managed care plan (although it is wise to periodically obtain quotations from multiple carriers and consider plan design changes). What I am talking about are tax-advantaged health insurance plans specifically designed by the federal government to make benefits more affordable for small employers.

These plans allow employees to pay with pre-tax dollars, which translates to more take-home pay. Bigger paychecks thrill employees. In addition, the savings make it easier for employers to cost-shift a great percentage of premiums to employees, if they choose to.

The plans you want to learn more about include: Cafeteria Plans (also called Section 125 plans, after the applicable tax code), Medical Savings Accounts (MSAs), and Health Saving Accounts (HSAs). All of these allow employees to pay for benefits and services with pre-tax dollars. And they're not just for medical expenses, but dental, vision, and other ancillary coverages. The broader you structure the plan, the greater the savings for you and your employees. Remember, every dollar your employee deposits in a pre-tax benefit plan is one less dollar you have to pay payroll-related taxes on.

If your workforce is composed of young, healthy employees, you might also want to investigate self-insured health plans. Self-insurance can translate to huge savings for groups that don't file many claims.

Sadly, many small employers shy away from these plans because they don't understand them and don't want to take the time to learn something new. Believe me, this is time well spent. These tax-advantaged plans were designed just for small employers. Knowledge is power. Put your insurance agent to work—and if he or she isn't up to the task, find one who is.

How about Barter Benefits?

One of the advantages of being small is that you can be creative in your approach to compensation and benefits. Earlier, we talked about unusual incentives you can offer your employees—how you can actually personalize compensation to hit your employee's individual hot buttons.

If your business lends itself to bartering, consider joining a barter association and turning those association dollars into personalized benefits for employees. How do you know if barter will work for you? Generally, if your business earns a reasonable gross profit or features a disappearing asset—such as hotel rooms—it may lend itself to bartering.

Barter, of course, is one of the oldest forms of commerce. Join a barter association, and you can trade your excess inventory or capacity for the goods and services offered by other association members. All transactions are managed by the barter association, which keeps track of your company's trade credits.

For example, a number of Chicago-based PRO members belong to the Illinois Trade Association. They have parlayed their surpluses into trade credits, which they use to purchase everything from printing services to vacations to gourmet meals to haircuts to furniture for their homes. Some members have taken this one step further, distributing trade credits among their employees—a unique benefit that costs them next to nothing.

Employees greatly enjoy spending their trade credits on little luxuries they would otherwise probably forgo—or practical expenses, such as braces for their kids.

Barter benefits are fun for employees and, because they're unique, make them feel like they're part of something special. And isn't that what benefit programs are supposed to do?

ENHANCING EMPLOYEE ATTITUDE

A happy employee is a productive employee. Since employees are so essential to your success, it's in your best interest to attend to their happiness. That means gauging attitudes on a regular basis and taking steps to boost morale. There are many ways to keep your people looking on the sunny side.

Watch Out for Organization Destroyers

Every employer has to be wary of subversive employees—the ones who, one way or another, chip away at the organization. Organization destroyers are particularly lethal in small companies, because their impact is more widely felt.

So, who are the number one organization destroyers? You may be surprised.

- It's not the underperformer who is absent as often as she's present.
- It's not the guy who spends too much time cruising the Internet.
- It's not even the unpopular bigmouth who people avoid.

No, the number one most destructive employee is that very qualified, dependable performer with the pervasively rotten attitude. Oh, she (or he) gets her work done just fine. In fact, she may be that long-term "expert," your company's resident go-to girl (or guy). She's the one who—through a litany of insidious criticisms—is destroying your other employees' morale. Listen carefully, and you'll hear constant criticisms of the customers, the company, and undoubtedly, you. She's poison!

This type of employee is hard to root out, because she does perform well and you count on her. Once you've recognized her true nature, it's tricky to confront her, because her performance is not at issue. But if you allow her toxins to fill the air, you'll find other employees slacking off, acting out, or quietly leaving. You need to call her (or him) on it. And if you can't get her to change her behavior—and this can be hard, since it's part of her nature—you have to be ready to let her go, expertise or not. These kinds of employees are just too destructive to keep around.

CASE STUDY: DESMOND

Desmond owns a company that services office equipment. For quite a long time, his number one technician was a very difficult man named Gary. Grumpy Gary was highly qualified and dealt adequately with customers, but he made Desmond's staff miserable. His incessant bullying and criticisms dragged the entire company down. One employee even left the company, reputedly because of Gary.

Because Gary was such a good service tech, Desmond was reluctant to terminate him. But even after repeated warnings, Gary would not modify his bad behavior.

Finally, Desmond let Gary go. He expected morale to pick up a bit, but he was surprised by how dramatically his employees responded. They were gratified that he cared enough about them to take action. And once morale rose, productivity did, too.

Using Outside Evaluations

If you really want to get the inside scoop on your employees' attitudes, consider using an outside consultant to do it. Employees are more likely to open up to a third party. Furthermore, outside experts, such as labor or HR consultants, have developed ways for getting the job done, like one-on-one interviews and anonymous questionnaires.

The goal is to surface misconceptions and areas of dissatisfaction so you can make improvements and shore up weak areas. Don't necessarily wait until you have a problem to conduct an evaluation. Some PRO members do this periodically as a proactive preventative measure.

But a word of caution: if you're like some of our members, the results may distress, shock, and/or anger you. "My people don't appreciate all I do for them!" is a common post-evaluation response.

Be prepared—but don't let this deter you if you think an evaluation might be valuable. No news isn't good news. Ignorance isn't bliss. Learn the truth so you can move forward.

Maximizing Employee Communications

Your employees are your first and most important customer. If you can't sell them on your company and its offerings, how will you sell anyone else?

Most entrepreneurs are used to working independently. That's just fine when you're a one-man operation, but not once you have a staff. Take pains to keep employees in the loop through ongoing communications about everything from changes in products and procedures to new strategies and objectives to new customers to regular sales results and achievements. Restate your vision and objectives often. Make sure everyone is aware of your goals and policies. And don't forget employee news, which everyone enjoys reading.

You can communicate through a variety of media, including newsletters (email makes it easy), flyers, announcements, and companywide meetings. The more you do it, the better you'll get at it.

Why take the trouble? For one thing, your employees will be better informed and therefore better able to do their job within the context of the organization. For another, you'll make them feel like an important part of your team, which is potent motivation.

Get Behind the Grill

Having a company picnic? Take it upon yourself—and your managers—to get behind the grill and serve up some employee appreciation, while giving your team a sizzlin' good time. Such gestures are powerful ways to let employees know that you value their contribution. It's fun and it's a great way to level the field, if only for a day.

Whenever you have a company event, make sure to circulate and spend time with as many people as possible. Even if it's an annual event, making personal connections with your employees will generate year-round benefits. Show your employees that they don't just work for you, you also work for them.

CASE STUDY: JOANNE

Joanne's company sells childproofing equipment. When the company makes its quota, Joanne invites her employees to her home, puts on her chef's apron, and serves them up a feast.

By waiting on her employees, Joanne makes them feel valued and special. She helps them feel like they're part of a family. In return, her employees are willing to go the extra mile for her year round. When Joanne fires up the oven, she also fires up her employees' loyalty.

Business owners who value their employees have an edge over those who do not. As a company grows, its staff becomes increasingly important to its success. Never fail to treat your number one asset with care and respect. Your company's future is in their hands.

CHAPTER SEVEN

INNOVATION AND IMPLEMENTATION

Change is occurring faster than ever in business today, due to advances in technology and distribution as well as increasing globalization. It's not enough to cope with change; you need to be able to take advantage of it. That requires innovation and the implementation of it.

Darwin was right. In order to survive, you need to continually adapt to meet the challenges of your environment. If you're not willing and able to change, your company will wind up like the dinosaurs—extinct.

THE NECESSITY OF CHANGE

In a competitive marketplace, the object is to continually render your product or service obsolete. In other words, you should be constantly looking for ways to improve your products or services—not to mention processes and systems—in order to outpace the competition. And that means getting your employees in on the act.

Does Your Culture Encourage Innovation?

How do you approach the prospect of change in your company? If you're like most entrepreneurs, you will say you're always open to new ideas. After all, you're reading this book, aren't you?

But the real proof of the pudding lies not in you, but in your company's culture. Does your culture activity court innovative thinking—not just pay lip service to it, but truly seek it out? Take the following quick quiz.

DOES YOUR CORPORATE CULTURE CULTIVATE INNOVATIVE THINKING?

- Do you periodically invite employees to submit suggestions and improvements, asking specifically for ideas on saving time, reducing paperwork, etc.?
- Do you have a process in place by which employees can submit their ideas—like a suggestion box or a designated email address?
- At meetings, do you encourage employees to share their thoughts?
- When your employees do make a suggestion, what's your very first, knee-jerk response? Do you welcome the idea—or find a reason to gently shoot it down?
- Do you reward and recognize employees for suggestions that are implemented?

All of these actions foster a culture of innovation. If you don't do them, start now. Consider expanding your employees' job descriptions to include responsibility for innovative thinking. Sometimes it's even advisable to go along with a crummy suggestion (assuming it doesn't hurt the business) in the name of fostering an innovative culture. It's that important.

Remember, your employees are the ones who have to walk through your processes and who are on the front lines with customers. They have great insights about the way things get done in your company. They know what's working and what isn't, whether they're conscious of it or not. It's your job to make them conscious—by creating a culture that stimulates creative thinking and encourages the sharing of those ideas.

The Pain of Change

Change is uncomfortable. Change is hard. When you make a change, you run the risk of failure. Some people are comfortable with change—a few even seek it out—but most of us resist it. And that undoubtedly applies to most of your employees, too.

How many times have you heard "But we've always done it this way!" either spoken aloud or implied in an employee's resistance to suggested change? As your company's leader, it's your job to continually challenge the status quo—something we talked about back in chapter 1. In contrast, most managers feel that their job is to *maintain* the status quo, to make sure things are done according to plan. As the high priests of processes and procedures, managers do not generally embrace innovation with wild abandon.

In fact, you might find more resistance to change in your managers than you do in employees who are lower down the hierarchy. After all, they have less to lose! It's often easier to make changes from the bottom up.

Be conscious of this natural resistance. Remind your people that the pain of change is less than the pain of staying the same. After all, what is more painful than extinction?

Evolution, Not Revolution

The world is constantly changing, and in order to survive—let alone profit—your company must change along with it. Think back. How much has your world changed over the last two decades? Remember little neighborhood hardware stores? They've all but disappeared, replaced by big-box home improvement giants. So have many mom-and-pop coffee shops, gone by way of Starbucks.

Remember telegrams from Western Union? First, telegrams gave way to fax machines...now faxes have largely been replaced by emails. Today, when you think of Western Union, you think about wiring money. Western Union was smart—it evolved to keep pace with the times.

These changes didn't happen overnight. The healthiest kind of company change is a gradual, constant evolution—not a drastic revolution. Continuously reinventing your company is preferable to a dramatic reengineering.

For one thing, you, the employer, are not taking as large a gamble. Constant evolution gives you the chance to see how the marketplace reacts to the changes you're implementing. All-out revolution, should it fail, can be fatal.

For another thing, it's easier on your organization to make small, continuous changes. It's easier on your cash flow, your processes, and most important, your employees. Employees can be devastated by overwhelming changes. But if employees are accustomed to working in a state of ongoing improvement, they become more accepting of new ideas. They learn that adapting is part of the job.

The speed of change, of course, is relative to your particular industry, and some move much faster than others. Regardless, if you stay on top of your industry by making routine enhancements, you can avoid the necessity of an earth-shattering reengineering.

View your company as a work in progress, and teach your employees to do so as well. Evolution isn't painful when it's part of your ongoing culture.

IMPLEMENTATION

Many great ideas have fallen by the wayside due to faulty implementation. The way you implement change can determine its success or failure. Remember the adage "the proof is in the pudding"? Well, no one will eat your pudding unless you cook it just right!

Innovation vs. Process

Have you noticed that there is a constant tension between innovation and process? Innovation, in the form of new ideas, leads to change. Process, on the other hand, maintains the status quo—the antithesis of change. Process is, in fact, repeating previously defined actions to get the same results you've gotten before.

When you implement an innovation, you create upheaval. Basically, you disrupt your processes—and that means taking a risk. For example, if you've ever updated your computer system, you know how such an improvement can wreak temporary havoc on your entire organization, creating all kinds of unintended consequences.

You can minimize the risk of failure by planning—in detail—the way you will implement an innovation once you've decided it's the right course of action. PRO members have found that the best way to plan is to bring employees on board in advance. In other words, before implementing a change, ask them to brainstorm all the possible issues that need to be addressed, as well as solutions. Your department managers know best how your proposed change will impact their specific area's workflow.

PRO member Joan uses a technique she calls "Pass the Solution" to get the most from her employees' collective brainpower. Here's how it works. Pose an issue. Say, for example, you want to upgrade your computer software with the least possible disruption. Direct every team member to write down every foreseeable snafu, along with possible solutions for each. Once everyone has identified problems and solutions, ask them to pass their sheets of paper to the person on their right.

Now a new pair of eyes can review the data—challenging, verifying, and refining it. Keep passing the papers along, until people stop writing. That means your issues have been well covered.

Finally, have the group prioritize the problems and rate the solutions. Now you have a binder full of specific ideas, a veritable guidebook to help you implement your innovation successfully.

Change Champions

We've already addressed that most human beings resist change. And chances are your employees are no exception. Once you've identified the need for change and charted your new direction, how do you get your employees to embrace it?

One way is to enforce change from the top down. Like the old shampoo commercial, you tell your staff, and they tell their staff, and so on. But chances are, somewhere not very far down the line, your employees will become resentful at having change forced upon them.

As an alternative, you might identify those employees who are not adverse to change and designate them your change champions. First, form a workgroup of change-receptive employees. Ask them to identify problems within the organization. Assign them the task of brainstorming viable solutions. Through your instructions, plant the seeds of the changes you desire, and then let them bring it to fruition.

Now, the proposed changes will be perceived as a positive, voluntary step conceived by the employees themselves—not as a top-down order. What a difference that perception will make!

Still think the change process will be a tough sell? You can always hire a consultant to do your dirty work.

CASE STUDY: AL

Al, whose company manufacturers building components, wanted to upgrade to a computerized drafting system. The problem: in the past, his employees demonstrated strong resistance to such change.

This time, rather than launch an all-out conversion, Al quietly introduced the system to a few select, forward-thinking employees. He told them he wanted their input.

One such employee was the shop foreman, a no-nonsense guy highly respected by his peers. Impressed by the software, the shop foreman declared it would make everyone's job easier. Hearing this, the other employees embraced the system—something they would never have done without the foreman's endorsement.

Nothing stays the same, especially in today's business climate. If your company cannot adapt, it will become extinct. If your company is to grow, it needs to exist in a constant state of evolution. When it comes to continued success, change is the only constant.

CHAPTER EIGHT

FINANCE: MONEY— FIND IT, GET IT, KEEP IT

Your business can't grow—not to mention survive— unless your finances are sound. Don't limit your focus to the top of your profit and loss statement. The true test is your bottom line.

Your company's financial health is impacted by a number of factors. Some of these factors—cash flow, banking relationships, collection techniques—are often neglected until there's trouble. Don't wait until your company's ailing to give these your attention. To keep your finances healthy, practice good preventative medicine.

CASH FLOW

It's not enough to have a positive P&L statement. Unless your cash flow is positive, your business is doomed. Let's look at some strategies for monitoring and managing cash flow, overcoming tough situations, and making sure your customers do their part to keep the cash rolling in.

Performing Cash Flow Projections

Many small employers tend not to think much about their cash flow until there's a problem with it. Of course, by then the horse is miles away from the stable.

That is why many PRO members routinely monitor cash flow and create cash flow projections. For one thing, it's a good way to gauge the company's health. For another, it can help you avoid getting caught shorthanded.

To get a handle on cash flow, ask yourself these questions:

- How much cash do I have right now?
- What are my payables (including aging)?
- What are my receivables (including aging)?
- What's my backlog—orders that have been received but not yet filled?

Then plot and trend these figures on a graph, which makes it easy to see where you're headed. Plot dates on one axis and cash on the other, and the picture becomes clear.

Plot Your Cash Flow!

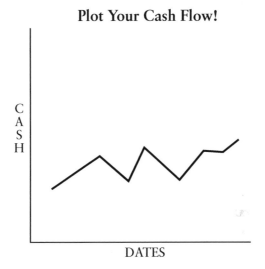

A word to the wise: one way to protect your cash flow is to avoid funding long-term investments with short-term monies or out of your current funds. If necessary, take out a loan, but do not use your operating funds.

It's easy to get so caught up in running the business that you forget to run the business wisely. Know your cash flow—and protect it.

Managing by Cash Flow to Get Out of Trouble

When business is good, it makes sense to manage the business by profit. But when you're thrown into a loss position, managing by cash flow can help you get back on solid ground.

For example, PRO member George suddenly and unexpectedly lost his largest customer, which not only constricted his cash flow but left him with too much inventory. Anne's company, on the other hand, grew so quickly that the company found itself in a negative cash position. Expenses like inventory, staff, and receivables skyrocketed. While her P&L looked good, she found herself with little cash on hand.

The solution for both of them? Manage by cash flow.

What this means is to track the way cash flows in and out of your business from month to month—and then "go with the flow." Identify what you have and what you need, and then focus your efforts on bringing in enough cash to cover your cash needs.

Both George and Anne employed multiple strategies to create cash flow. These included:

- Reducing inventory.
- Establishing/increasing credit with their banks.
- Reducing receivables through aggressive collection practices.
- Reducing perceived fixed expenses, such as rent and advertising expenses.

By managing cash flow in a disciplined way, both were able to steadily improve their position over time.

Getting the Most from a Financial Loss

Even the most savvy business owner can have a bad year. When you find yourself dealing with a loss, you might as well take advantage of it. Take advantage of it? You bet!

The smart thing to do is to maximize the loss by writing off everything you can. Personally, you might find this difficult, but it usually makes sense financially and it can help clear the decks for your future profitability.

Here's the secret. An often overlooked section of tax code allows businesses to "carry back" a financial loss for up to three prior tax years. This means you can use the loss to recalculate your tax liability for the past three years and recoup some or all of the taxes you paid.

For example, PRO member Charlene had an admittedly bad year, thanks to disappointing sales and larger-than-expected R&D expenses. Rather than try to minimize her loss, she took a deep breath and "cleared the decks." This meant:

- Liquidating excess inventory by selling it at a low price.
- Expensing R&D instead of capitalizing it.
- Postponing sales until the following tax year, when able.

The end result? Charlene got all her negatives out of the way, better positioning herself for a profitable year ahead.

A word of caution: before proceeding in this direction, talk to your accountant, attorney, and banker. Carrying back a tax loss generally will make your business appear weaker. You don't want to worry your lender, nor do you want to violate your covenant with your bank. See if your loan has a net-worth provision. If you stand to break it, consider all the angles before taking action.

Avoiding Bankruptcy with an "Informal 11"

What do you do if you've exhausted your credit and you're really in trouble? One way to avoid bankruptcy is to quietly declare what we call an "Informal 11." Over the years, we've had two PRO members who used this strategy successfully, enlisting the aid of their creditors to circumvent bankruptcy.

What do you do? Swallow your pride and meet with each of your creditors, one-on-one. Tell them quite honestly that you're in trouble. Tell them that you do want to pay them. Ask them to reduce your debt or present them with a payment schedule that you can meet and to honor new orders on a COD basis. Remind them that if you do go into bankruptcy, they will get very little.

Our PRO members were relieved and pleased to find their creditors willing to "get a haircut" (take something off the top). The vendors acknowledged that getting something is better than getting nothing. They were willing to work something out as an investment against the future. Both our stories had a happy ending. After about two years, our members were able to work their way out of debt and pay back their creditors.

Yes, this really can be done. The key is to be completely honest with your creditors and your bank. Remember, your credibility is all you have. And don't procrastinate, no matter how hard it is. Get everyone on board as early as possible. No one likes surprises, especially bankers and creditors. But they don't want to see their customers fail, either, especially with outstanding debt.

Dealing with a Customer's Questionable Credit

So you have the chance to acquire a new desirable customer but that customer's credit is less than perfect. You want the business, but you don't want to make a bad decision. Do you take a chance, or do take a pass?

The answer depends largely on how your business is structured—i.e., your gross profit percentage. Remember, if your customer doesn't pay his bills, your true loss is the actual cost of goods sold. The higher your gross margin, the greater the risk you can afford to take. The lower your gross margin, the more cautious you should be, because a potential loss represents a greater cost to your company.

Either way, if you don't take that customer's business, you can lose as well—you lose a hundred percent of potential sales and profit. So how do you make an intelligent decision? By determining the true variable cost— your actual risk. Gather as much information as possible about your potential customer's credit history. Request a Dun & Bradstreet report or a consumer credit score. Ask the customer to provide a bank reference. Learn as much as you can. Ask yourself, *Can I afford to take this risk? What may this relationship be worth to you?*

Sometimes you can do all these things and still emerge without a clear course of action. In that case, yes, you can still take on the customer, but sell to him on a COD basis, at least for starters. Give him a chance to prove himself.

Or do what some PRO members do: offer to sell on a consignment basis. In the auto industry, manufacturers often provide dealers with three months of "free flooring." If the car hasn't sold after three months, the manufacturer begins charging interest. You can still structure a similar arrangement.

One word of caution: if you do sell on consignment, have your sales reps check the inventory on a regular basis. Advise the customer that you will be visiting regularly to match his inventory against what he ordered. You want to make sure that no items go AWOL and that there are no discrepancies.

As I've said before, risk is necessary for growth. Yes, you can and should take some risks like these. Just be sure to measure them first.

Fresh Collection Strategies

Most small businesses have their share of collection headaches. Most rely on collection agencies and attorneys to deal with delinquent customers.

One of the advantages of owning a small business is that you can try unconventional collection strategies without going through layers of management approval. After all, you *are* management! Over the years, PRO members have come up with some fairly innovative strategies to collect what is owed them, including the following.

- *Have a heart-to-heart*—Meet with the customer, get to the heart of the problem, and set up a workable payment schedule. Earlier in this chapter, we talked about structuring an "Informal 11" when your company is in trouble. Why not use the same idea—in reverse—for customers in the same boat? Something is better than nothing. And chances are you will win your customer's undying gratitude for offering a positive solution.

- *Barter*—Think creatively. In lieu of cash, can the customer pay you in goods or services?
- *Scare 'em*—Threaten to tarnish the customer's name throughout the industry by announcing its delinquency. This is a tough approach that won't lay the groundwork for a future relationship, but it can be effective. (If your industry offers a vehicle for sharing such information, participate. For example, credit managers in some manufacturing markets regularly pool data. No customer wants to be blacklisted by an entire industry!)
- *Take a credit card*—If you accept credit cards, suggest the customer transfer his balance onto one and pay it off via his credit card company. Then delinquent payments become the customer's problem, not yours.
- *Give a discount*—Offer the customer an immediate 5 to 10 percent discount if he or she pays you off right away. The discount will be offset by the time and energy you will save in your collection efforts.
- *Recover your product*—Offer to take back all merchandise that hasn't been sold to shrink the bill.
- *Take it upstairs*—Take your complaint to the highest level of the company.

Don't limit yourself to traditional collection strategies. A little creativity can go a long way.

CASE STUDY: KEN

Ken's company sells air compressors. He sold one to a customer who, after it was delivered, claimed he couldn't afford to pay for it. Months went by, and Ken had no success collecting from this customer.

Then the air compressor broke. The impossibly nervy customer called Ken, insisting Ken honor his warranty and repair the machine, even though it hadn't been paid for yet.

Ken could have told this customer to forget it. Instead, he shrewdly agreed to honor the warranty and fix the machine—provided that the customer hand the service tech the payment check the moment he arrived. Case closed.

BANKING RELATIONSHIPS

Many small business owners are reluctant to borrow money. But if you want to grow your business, you'll undoubtedly need more money to support your expanding inventory, accounts receivable, fixed assets, etc. You have three choices: invest more capital, borrow the money, or hold down growth. Contrary to what you may think, borrowing is not a bad thing. Bank loans allow you to grow without taking on an equity partner. Your banker is your friend!

Know Your Lending Officer (and His Boss)

Your banker plays an important role in your company's growth. Treat him or her well, the same way you would treat a favorite customer. Get to know your banker and make sure he or she knows you. Touch base regularly and cultivate a relationship, keeping him or her up-to-date on your business. Don't wait until you have a problem; create credibility for yourself every chance you get.

In addition, make a point of meeting your banker's manager. Banking is not like the old days, when you would deal with the same person for life. There's movement in relationship managers. Of course, the higher up a person is in the hierarchy, the less likely they are to leave. So contacts with upper management will serve you well if your immediate contact gives notice.

Besides, loans are approved—not by individuals—but by internal committees. When you have a loan up for approval, you want as many people as possible on your side. And speaking of loans, don't be afraid to take one! The fact is, most small businesses don't generate enough dollars to fund real growth. Sooner or later, you will need a loan. That's why you have a banker in the first place, isn't it?

At PRO, we recognize that it's important for small businesses to develop key resources. Your banker is one of them.

How to Communicate Negative Information

No one likes being the bearer of bad news. But no one likes being the recipient, either—and that includes your banker. However, if your company is in trouble, keeping it a secret is the worst thing you can do. How do you make the best of a bad situation?

Your mother was right: honesty is the best policy. As we discussed earlier, you have no choice but to share the news with your banker. But whatever you do, don't burst in, pour your heart out, and throw yourself at your banker's knees. Instead, carefully plan what you're going to say and do, following the four-point strategy used by PRO members.

1. *Be honest, professional, and specific.* Share your numbers, including sales and expenses. Explain any pertinent market conditions as well.

2. *Be ready to explain why your numbers are off.* Has a new competitor lured away some key accounts? Have you had production issues in the factory? This exercise forces you to identify your company's problems.

3. *Rather than wring your hands, offer a viable plan for remedying the problem*—a concrete action plan that you've thought out in advance. If you want some help from your banker, be ready to articulate your request in specific terms. You need to know what you want to ask for!

4. *Project confidence.* If you've addressed your problems and are working to fix them, you have a right to a can-do attitude. Don't act like a loser—chances are you'll be taken at your word.

Project Your Needs: Don't Work Hand-to-Mouth

Want to ask your bank for a loan? You may be tempted to ask for the absolute minimum you need. Don't! Think it through before you open your mouth.

As a small business owner, you want to be proactive, not reactive. Project your needs for a given period—say, at least a year—before requesting a loan. Take the long view, and avoid the habit of working hand to mouth. It's not only smarter for your business; it demonstrates to your banker that you know your business.

For example, PRO member George wanted to buy a new press for his print shop—a press that would allow him to take on new projects he couldn't previously accommodate. He was all set to ask his bank for a loan in the amount of the press. Luckily, his PRO group stopped him in time!

Why? Because it wasn't enough to simply cover the cost of the press. In order to get those lucrative new projects, George would have to get the word out to customers. That would mean investing in an advertising campaign, marketing materials, and some additional training for his print brokers. George wisely increased the size of the loan to pay for these related items (which, by the way, insured that the press would start paying for itself more quickly).

All that being said, sometimes things happen that can't be anticipated. Perhaps a rare opportunity comes your way. Perhaps an unforeseen problem surfaces. One of the advantages of small business is flexibility. If changing conditions—and not poor planning—calls for a second loan, that doesn't mean you can't go for it.

MISCELLANEOUS ISSUES

Unlike senior corporate executives, small business owners are personally involved with every aspect of their company. When it comes to financial challenges, they deal with them on a more personal level. Let's address some of these thornier issues, as well as solutions for handling them.

When Do You Cut a Customer Off?

There are some customers that simply can't or won't pay their bills the way they should. And no matter how much they buy or how prestigious they are, at some point you must consider cutting them off.

Most small business owners have a hard time refusing to sell a customer any more product. In many ways, it goes against the grain. But, emotions aside, sometimes it's the right thing to do. How do you know when that time is?

PRO members have spent many hours debating this tricky subject. In the end, we developed a list of factors to help guide us through this agonizing decision.

- *The Hassle Factor*—How much time are you and your staff regularly wasting in collection efforts? There's an old expression that says "If your friends have fleas, you have fleas." Is your team itching and scratching over this account? Or can you redefine your rules to resolve the hassle?

- *Trust*—Trust is necessary to a healthy business relationship. Is your trust in this customer permanently eroded? Can you correct the misunderstanding and move forward?
- *Gross Margin Contribution*—If you operate with a high gross margin (i.e., a healthy mark-up) you are in a better position to wait for your money. The less risk you have, the longer you can wait. Remember, the potential loss here is not lost revenues, it's the cost of goods sold and the time spent managing the account.
- *Your Lender*—Is your bank including receivables as a basis for funding? If you have an asset-based loan, late payers are particularly problematic. When calculating assets, most lenders will not include receivables that have aged ninety days.
- *Leverage*—How much leverage do you have with your customer? If you're providing a hard-to-find product or service, you have heavy-duty bargaining power. Leverage it to facilitate payment.

Once you've weighed these factors, you are in a better position to make a practical decision. If you've decided not to cut the customer off, make every effort to work the problems out. In the meantime, seriously consider restricting new sales to COD only.

If you are ready to pull the plug, you can always take the customer to small claims court. Too high a hassle factor? Write the loss off as an invaluable lesson learned, and don't lose any sleep over it.

Loaning Money to Your Company? Protect Yourself!

Most PRO members have loaned money to their businesses at one point or another. Chances are you will someday do the same, so you must know how to protect yourself.

First, make sure those dollars are legally viewed as a *loan,* not *equity.* (When banks calculate debt-to-equity ratios, owner loans are considered equity.) Then, have your attorney draw up a note designating you a secured lender, and be sure to file all necessary UCC (Uniform Commercial Code) documents.

These legal maneuvers will protect you in the event of bankruptcy or liquidation. If you've made your company a business loan, you want the investment to be treated like one—not a capital loss. And of course you want to be paid before other creditors.

There is a hierarchy to bankruptcy payments. Secured loans are repaid first, followed by unsecured loans, and finally, equity. By defining yourself as a secured lender, you move your loan near the top of the hierarchy, just below bank loans.

A word to the wise: if you're seeking money through your bank, your banker may encourage you to take out a home equity loan and route it through your business. Don't do it! Take the home equity loan out individually, and then fund the business yourself using the above-described steps. Otherwise, should the business fail, you could literally lose your home, too.

The idea of a future bankruptcy may appear highly

unlikely, not to mention disturbing. But one never knows. Take the trouble to protect your funds.

Your finances won't take care of themselves. Even if you're not a numbers person, force yourself to put some basic controls in place. Monitor your cash flow, cultivate a good relationship with your banker, and stay on top of delinquent customers. If you do run into problems, address them immediately. When it comes to your company's financial health, an ounce of prevention is worth a pound of cure.

CHAPTER NINE

SUCCESSION AND TRANSITION

Each person's activity in a business has a beginning and an end. Believe it or not, that includes you. Most people don't like to think about the latter, but it truly is necessary. This is something that will deeply affect your family, your business, and most of all, yourself.

Even if you're decades away from retirement, it pays to start planning now. Having a succession plan and exit strategy, even sketchy ones, will help you make better decisions along the way—decisions that will ease that future transition and protect your company. Remember, we're talking about your life here!

HAVING A LIFE PLAN

Where do you see yourself five, ten, even twenty-five years from now? How do you plan on getting there?

As the Cheshire cat said, "If you don't know where you're going, any road will take you there." Don't make the mistake that Alice did. Take time to map your life.

Make an Appointment with Your Life

For most small business owners, there's not much of a gap between one's business and personal life. When you own a business, the workday rarely ends at 5:00 p.m. It's pretty much with you 24/7.

That's why it's so important to love what you do—and to be ready to move on when that's no longer the case. You should periodically ask yourself, *Am I happy? Healthy? Stimulated? Miserable?* It's important to weigh the role of the business in your life against your other priorities—health, family, leisure, travel, and all your non-work-related goals.

If you admit to yourself that you just aren't happy in the business, ask yourself if there is a way to fix it. If there isn't, it's time to plan your exit. Now.

Ah, but what if you're happy in your business? What if you can't imagine life without it? Guess what—it's still time to start thinking about an exit plan!

Ideally, every business owner should have his or her exit plan in place from the very early days of the business. Realistically, that's rarely the case. Remember, some exit strategies take years to implement. That's why it's important to think about it now.

What about the Kids?

Some small business owners are lucky enough to have capable children who grow up in the company and are eager to someday take over the reins. Others don't. Not all owners are qualified to be managers—a fact to keep in mind when evaluating your children's future role in your business.

No matter how much you love your offspring, if you don't think they have what it takes to someday run the business, resist the urge to bring them on board. Of course, sometimes you won't know for sure until it's too late. Then what?

One of our PRO members, John, spent months agonizing over this issue. He had brought his son Dennis into the business, only to discover that Dennis wasn't remotely suited for it. Yet he resisted the thought of "firing" his fair-haired boy—even though, when it came to the business, his heir was more rightly named Dennis the Menace.

Ultimately, at the gentle urging of his fellow members, he offered his son a generous severance plan, with two years full salary. That, he explained, would allow Dennis plenty of time to find a more suitable career. By offering such a generous pay-off, he not only saved their father/son relationship, he saved the company's future.

Do You Have a Successor?

Right now—today—do you have a likely successor among your employees? Someone who could step in and run the business in your absence?

Should you choose to retire while maintaining owner-ship, you're going to need a sharp, loyal successor to keep your business running profitably. And should you decide to sell the business to an employee, that person is going to need to be capable in order to be able to pay you. There are many smart reasons to start grooming a suc-cessor now, even if retirement is decades away.

Your best candidate may not necessary be your highest-ranking employee. Your successor should display the lead-ership, vision, and communication skills we've been talking about throughout this book, or at least have the potential to develop them.

That's a tall order. So if you'd like a successor, you need to find one and start a comprehensive grooming process—one that includes providing training, feedback, and opportunities for growth. And of course, before you invest too much energy in grooming a candidate, you're going to have to make sure that person is potentially interested in the position.

If you don't have an employee who fits the bill, keep this in mind as you make future hires. Knowing your exit strategy will help you make the better hire to help you accomplish your long-term goals (i.e., choosing an "intre-preneur" vs. an entrepreneur, as we discussed earlier).

Taking the Vacation Test

Taking an extended vacation—say, three or four weeks off—is a great way to test both yourself and your organization in terms of your "exit readiness." That time spent away from the office will tell you many things about yourself. Are you constantly resisting the urge to call? Or do you enjoy the freedom from daily work demands? Do you return raring to get back to work—or are you already looking forward to your next big break?

Your responses can tell you how close you are to retirement readiness. Your staff's performance in your absence tells you how ready your company is to pick up the slack.

Does business take place as usual without you? Or is it one unresolved crisis after another? Who keeps the business going? Have you properly defined and delegated responsibility and authority? If things didn't go well in your absence, identify the weaknesses and use this as an opportunity to shore them up.

You should be able to take an extended vacation without all hell breaking loose. Make it one of your goals— it's healthy for both you and your company.

CASE STUDY: WILLIAM

William took a three-week trip to Europe. He had never been away from the office for so long, and he was apprehensive about leaving beforehand.

- The first week, he called in every single day. Everything was fine.
- The second week, he called in every other day. Everything was fine.

- The third week, he never called in at all. And that was fine with William.
- The upshot: both William and his company are "exit-ready." Good job!

EXIT STRATEGIES

Having an exit strategy doesn't necessarily mean that you're leaving the business. It might mean having the right people in place in order to make your future life easier. Whether you wish to someday sell your business or keep it in the family, knowing your exit strategy allows you to make better decisions, positioning your company for the future.

Developing Your Exit Strategy

Surely you have a general idea of what you think may happen someday. Will you sell the business? Turn it over to your children? Promote yourself to Chairman of the Board so you can enjoy semiretirement while still having a place to hang your hat?

"I don't have time to think about this now!" you may say. "That's way down the road. I have more important decisions to make right now."

Ah...that's where you're wrong. Your exit strategy, no matter what it is or when it will happen, should impact the decisions you're making today.

Take, for example, your hiring process. If you long to be Chairman of the Board someday, you'll want to start grooming an "intrepreneur" who can ably run every facet of your business, yet has no desire to own it. On the other hand, if you plan to sell someday, you'll want someone with more entrepreneurial drive, someone who will happily take over your business.

Similarly, decisions like taking on new projects and investments should be weighed in light of your exit strategy. If you plan to work in the business for another twenty years, you have a higher tolerance for such risk. But if you're planning to leave five years from now, will you want to take on something new?

Life is to be lived. To the best of my knowledge, we only get one turn. Make sure you're living the life of your choice. Don't shy away from creating a succession plan and exit strategy, because these are the vehicles that will take you where you want to go.

The decisions you make today will position your company for tomorrow. When you have a map to follow, you know you're headed in the right direction.

CHAPTER TEN

DIAGNOSTIC TESTS

The following quick and easy diagnostic tests are designed to give you a snapshot assessment of your company's strengths and weaknesses. Essentially, each quiz contains a short checklist of the attributes your company's processes and disciplines should include.

These brief quizzes are far from comprehensive. However, they should be helpful in identifying your organization's key strengths, while pinpointing weaknesses so you can improve them.

For each quiz, simply circle "yes" or "no" for every question. To determine your score, give yourself one point for each "yes" answer and total your points. But don't just look at your total scores—go back and review each question that earned a "no" answer. In about sixty seconds, you can identify the areas you need to work on most.

Test #1: Overall Management and Organization

QUESTION	CIRCLE ONE

1. Is your market share increasing—or at least remaining level?

    Yes   No

2. Do you have measurable goals for your company?   Yes   No

3. Do you have an exit strategy or succession plan?   Yes   No

4. Does your company have a strategic plan and/or marketing plan?

    Yes   No

5. Do you encourage change within your organization? Yes   No

6. Is your company budget broken down (at the least) into quarters?

    Yes   No

7. Do you know your financial break-even point?   Yes   No

8. Do you have a vision or long-term objective for your company?

    Yes   No

9. Do you insist on above-average performance?   Yes   No

10. Do you believe your company may have to reinvent itself within the next three to five years?   Yes   No

Scoring: Give yourself one point for every "yes" answer.

9–10	Outstanding! You are doing a great job.
7–8	Good. However, proceed to the individual diagnostic tests to pinpoint areas of improvement.
5–6	Fair. You're not running your business—your business is running you! It is important to start making changes.
4 or less	Take action now…your business is in trouble!

Test #2: Sales and Sales Management

QUESTION	CIRCLE ONE	
1. Do you have a defined sales process?	Yes	No
2. Do you have a scripted sales presentation outline?	Yes	No
3. Do you know the personality profile of your successful salespeople?		
	Yes	No
4. Have you identified the key accounts to sell—current or new?		
	Yes	No
5. Do you have a sales training program (internal or external)?		
	Yes	No
6. Do you have written, measurable sales and activity objectives?		
	Yes	No
7. Do you measure sales activities and compare them to results?		
	Yes	No
8. Do you reward or incent the sales performance activities you desire?		
	Yes	No
9. Have you asked customers what "quality service" means to them?		
	Yes	No
10. Do you measure customer service performance?	Yes	No

Scoring: Give yourself one point for every "yes" answer.

9–10	Outstanding! You have a model sales organization.
7–8	Good. However, your sales process could benefit from some tweaking.
5–6	Fair. You need greater organization and structure in your sales organization.
4 or less	Take action now! Your sales structure, management, and format need immediate attention. Please refer to chapters 2 and 3.

Test #3: Marketing

QUESTION	CIRCLE ONE	
1. Do you have a marketing plan?	Yes	No
2. Do you have a quarterly or annual marketing budget?	Yes	No
3. Is your marketing budget broken down into budgeted tactics?	Yes	No
4. Have you defined your customer (do you know who your customer is)?	Yes	No
5. Do you have a differentiation statement?	Yes	No
6. Do you have at least one employee with defined marketing responsibilities?	Yes	No
7. Do you know your Unique Selling Proposition?	Yes	No
8. Do you measure your marketing results against a target and/or budget?	Yes	No
9. Do you outline a marketing communications plan every year?	Yes	No
10. Have you produced a brochure or other marketing materials or updated your website in the last year?	Yes	No

Scoring: Give yourself one point for every "yes" answer.

9–10	Outstanding! You are a world-class marketer.
7–8	Good. However, consider incorporating more proactive planning.
5–6	Fair. Your marketing process, management, and programs need more organization and structure.
4 or less	Take action now! It's not too late, but your marketing organization needs an immediate overhaul. Please refer to chapter 4.

Test #4: Operations

QUESTION	CIRCLE ONE

1. Do you define, track, and measure your company's key items of performance (e.g., delivery time, order fill percentage, rejects, etc.)?

    Yes   No

2. Do you have a budget and measure its variances?   Yes   No

3. When you have a negative variance, do you take corrective action?

    Yes   No

4. Do you know your capacity utilization by critical operational centers?

    Yes   No

5. Do you break your expenses into "fixed" and "variable"?

    Yes   No

6. Can you cite your break-even point?   Yes   No

7. Do you know the gross profit on each of your products/services—and do you track sales by these key areas?   Yes   No

8. Do you know your true costs?   Yes   No

9. Do your employees know what a "good job" consists of?

    Yes   No

10. Do your employees know your operations standards?

    Yes   No

Scoring: Give yourself one point for every "yes" answer.

9–10	Outstanding! You are an operations guru.
7–8	Good. However, you could still have a firmer handle on your business.
5–6	Fair. You really need to know what drives the profit and performance of your business.
4 or less	Take action now! You are not collecting the information you need to make informed decisions. Please refer to chapters 5 and 8.

Test #5: Human Resources

QUESTION	CIRCLE ONE	
1. Do your employees have written job descriptions?	Yes	No
2. Do you conduct formal employee evaluations?	Yes	No
3. Do you have objective measurements of performance?	Yes	No
4. Do you provide any type of employee recognition?	Yes	No
5. Do you have an employee handbook?	Yes	No
6. When an employee performs below average, do you take action?	Yes	No
7. Do you believe filling any open position is an opportunity to improve the organization?	Yes	No
8. Do you enforce progressive discipline with problem employees?	Yes	No
9. Do you communicate with employees (beyond word of mouth)?	Yes	No
10. Have you or your managers received training on how to conduct a new employee interview?	Yes	No

Scoring: Give yourself one point for every "yes" answer.

9–10	Outstanding! We bow to your HR wisdom.
7–8	Good. You appear to have good communication with your employees.
5–6	Fair. You need to do a better job telling your employees what is expected of them.
4 or less	Take action now! Your people are your key asset. You must maximize communication and enhance recruitment processes. Please refer to chapters 5 and 6.

Test #6: Compensation

QUESTION	CIRCLE ONE

1. Do your employees have measurable goals and objectives?

Yes   No

2. Are company compensation adjustments tied to performance?

Yes   No

3. Do your employees know if they are doing a good job?

Yes   No

4. Do your employees generally feel they are compensated fairly?

Yes   No

5. Do your employees appreciate their benefit programs?

Yes   No

6. Do you know how your compensation compares to other companies for jobs requiring similar skill levels?   Yes   No

7. Do you communicate with your employees regularly (at least annually), explaining the rationale for their compensation and how they can earn more?   Yes   No

8. Do you tell your employees the company's cost of their total benefits?

Yes   No

9. Do you know the percentage of the total benefit package compared to base wages?   Yes   No

10. Do you let employees know how the company is doing?

Yes   No

Scoring: Give yourself one point for every "yes" answer.

9–10	Outstanding! Your compensation methods are state-of-the-art.
7–8	Good. However, you could benefit from knowing more about how your compensation stacks up.
5–6	Fair. You need to do more work tying benefits to performance and communicating to employees.
4 or less	Take action now! Your company's approach to compensation needs a major overhaul.

Test #7: Finance

QUESTION	CIRCLE ONE	
1. Does your company have a written budget?	Yes	No
2. If so, is the budget broken down by areas of responsibility/cost centers?		
	Yes	No
3. Do you prepare cash flow projections?	Yes	No
4. Do you meet with your bank at least twice a year to discuss progress and problems?	Yes	No
5. Is your financial information timely?	Yes	No
6. Do you measure variances from the budget at least quarterly?		
	Yes	No
7. Do you measure and track your accounts receivable by number of days or outstanding or aged receivables?	Yes	No
8. When cash goes up or down, do you know why?	Yes	No
9. Do you know your break-even point?	Yes	No
10. Do you define, track, and measure your company's key items of performance and measure them? (e.g., customer complaints, accounts receivable days outstanding, inventory turnover ratio, etc.)		
	Yes	No

Scoring: Give yourself one point for every "yes" answer.

9–10	Outstanding! You are making the right financial moves.
7–8	Good. However, you could benefit from knowing more about what makes your business tick.
5–6	Fair. Are you running a rudderless ship? It's time to put controls in place.
4 or less	Take action now! With no controls, how do you make a profit? Please refer to chapter 8.

EPILOGUE

Now that you've reached the end of this book, don't put it away on a bookshelf somewhere. Put it to work for you instead!

Hopefully, these once pristine pages are now dog-eared and covered in sticky notes. Did you scribble in the margins? Excellent! That means you found some ideas worth noting.

As a small business owner, you have a responsibility to your company and employees, as well as your family and above all yourself. That responsibility? To be the best you can be. The aim of this book is to help you get there.

After all, the business world isn't standing still, and you can't afford to either. Use every tool at your disposal, including those offered here.

They say there's no substitute for experience. By sharing in the experiences of other small business owners—in this case, members of PRO advisory boards—you vicariously reap the benefits of their failures, triumphs, and lessons learned. I'm hoping you found solutions to some of your own business challenges or insights that will help you approach things in a whole new way. Needless to say, I'm also hoping you found reams of ideas that you're eager to adapt or try for yourself.

Perhaps you're also inspired to find your own peer group advisory board. If you found yourself stimulated by the stories in this book—if you have questions, observations, and experiences to share—then I urge you to look into it. Running a business is much easier (and more fun!) when you don't feel so alone at the top. The truth is, you don't have to be. And that, my friend, is the best secret of all.

INDEX

20% Rule, 141, 142

ABOUT THE AUTHOR

Ray Silverstein has been a small business expert for over three decades. He is president and founder of PRO (President's Resource Organization), a network of peer group advisory boards for small business owners. He facilitates PRO groups throughout metro Chicago and Phoenix, where entrepreneurs share ideas, problems, and solutions in order to better grow their businesses.

A recognized small business authority, Silverstein has been featured in numerous publications, including the *Wall Street Journal*, *Chicago Tribune*, *Crain's Chicago Business*, *Entrepreneur*, and *Inc*. He serves on small business panels and was the small business expert at the first Small Business Forum sponsored by the *Chicago Tribune*.

A former CEO twice over and a grower of businesses, Silverstein learned firsthand that it's "lonely at the top."

In addition to developing business-owner peer groups, he is committed to small business education. He has taught entrepreneurship at a Chicago area college and has developed several educational courses including "Taking Your Business to the Next Level" and "Ready, Set, Grow." He is also founder of the Institute for Small Business Success, a nonprofit organization that helps entrepreneurs achieve success through ongoing education.